The SSIS Catalog

Install, Manage, Secure, and Monitor your Enterprise ETL Infrastructure

Tim Mitchell

The SSIS Catalog

Install, Manage, Secure, and Monitor your Enterprise ETL Infrastructure

ISBN: 9798664282894

Credits

Publisher: Tyleris Data Solutions (Tyleris.com)

Author: Tim Mitchell

Technical Reviewers: Bill Fellows and Joshua Ferguson

Disclaimer

While the author(s) have taken care to ensure that the information and advice in this book is accurate, they make no representations or warranties of any kind for the content herein. Neither the publisher nor the author(s) shall be liable for any errors or omissions in this book.

Contact

For reprint rights or other inquiries, contact info@tyleris.com.

Table of Contents

About the Author

Tim Mitchell is a business intelligence architect, author, and trainer. He has been building data solutions for over 17 years, specializing in data warehousing, ETL/SSIS, and reporting. He holds a Bachelor's Degree in Computer Science from Texas A&M at Commerce, and has been recognized as a Microsoft Data Platform MVP each year since 2010. Tim is the founder and principal data architect at Tyleris Data Solutions, a consulting firm focused on delivering on-premises and cloud-based solutions on the Microsoft data platform.

As an active member of the community, Tim has spoken at international, regional, and local venues including the SQL PASS Summit, SQLBits, SQL Connections, SQL Saturday events, and various user groups and webcasts. Tim is coauthor of the book SSIS Design Patterns, and is a contributing author on the charity book project MVP Deep Dives 2. He is a member of the Boulder BI Brain Trust, a Melissa Data MVP, and is active in the North Texas SQL Server User Group in the Dallas area.

You can visit his website and blog at TimMitchell.net or follow him on Twitter at twitter.com/Tim_Mitchell.

About the Technical Reviewers

Bill Fellows is an author, consultant, and technology enthusiast living in the Kansas City area. Bill is the owner and principal architect at Sterling Data Consulting and a 4-time Microsoft Data Platform MVP awardee. He has been focused on data integration, design, and development since 1999. Bill blogs at http://billfellows.blogspot.com, and is on Twitter at @billinkc.

Joshua Ferguson is a senior consultant with Tyleris Data Solutions. He has a master's degree in Computer Science, and is currently living in Japan. Joshua is a skilled architect and technologist, working with everything from SQL Server and SSIS to Raspberry Pi. He is on Twitter at @_jwfergus.

Acknowledgements

Writing is often lonely work, but it's rarely a solo effort. Although it's just my name on the cover, I owe a debt of gratitude to the numerous folks who have contributed to the completion of this book.

I must first and foremost thank my wife Rachel for running interference for me while I borrowed what would have otherwise been relaxing family time to complete this book. She has been patient and accommodating well beyond what I have earned.

Thanks also to my kids for their patience. Ryan, Evan, and Kaylee have all been good sports about this project, even though (in Evan's words), "Dad's always in his office writing!"

Thanks to Bill Fellows and Joshua Ferguson for their careful attention during the technical review process, astutely pointing out my errors and omissions (of which were many, I assure you). For all of you budding authors out there, I can tell you that there are fewer things more valuable to a writer than an editor or reviewer who is unafraid of stepping on your toes.

I want to thank a few people who helped to guide me in my early days as a writer. Thanks to Steve Jones, editor at SQLServerCentral.com, who gave me my first paid writing opportunities. Also, thanks to Andy Warren, who was one of the first people I met after getting involved in the SQL Server community, and who has been to me a great source of encouragement and insight over the years. I owe a word of thanks as well to Andy Leonard, who was one of the first people to encourage me as a writer. Finally, thanks to my friend Mike Walsh, who was kind enough to give me a gentle nudge (and on occasion, a swift kick) when I fell behind on my writing schedule.

Introduction

I still remember when I discovered SQL Server Integration Services. It was sometime in 2006, and SSIS had been on the market for less than a year at that point. Data Transformation Services (DTS) was on its way out the door, giving way to the new and shiny features of SSIS.

Up to that point, my experience with moving and massaging data was limited to a handful of Perl and C# scripts that I had built with a lot of help from my friend Dr. Google. I fancied myself as more of a developer than a data guy back then, so I felt comfortable building lightweight data movement processes in code. The problem with this approach was that I had taken a new job the year before, and in that role I was tasked with building dozens of load processes that would collectively move hundreds of millions of rows of data. I knew my quick-and-dirty scripts wouldn't cut it.

I had attended the PASS Summit the prior year, and had heard a little about what SSIS was and what it did. When my new boss tapped me to build the extract-transform-load (ETL) process for a large application migration project, I fired up my developer copy of SQL Server 2005 and started building my first SSIS package. It didn't take me long to become enamored with this shiny new tool! What used to take me hours of scripting could be done much more quickly, in an easy-to-understand graphical environment.

Although those first SSIS packages I built were far from perfect, I managed to hack together a "just good enough" ETL process to get our big project over the finish line. Successful data projects tend to beget even more requests for data, so I slowly became the go-to guy for all my employer's data integration needs. This meant that I got to spend a lot more time using my new favorite tool, SSIS.

I did enjoy those early days of working with SSIS, but the longer I worked with it, the lengthier my wish list for it became. As I used SSIS more and more, I pondered the following:

- Why does it have to be so difficult to apply a configuration to a package? If I configure one package to execute another, I have to open both of them in the editor to make sure the parent/child configurations are set up properly, since SSIS won't enforce those relationships.

- Why can't we have more granular control over security for packages deployed to SQL Server?

- Does the logging of SSIS packages really need to be this cumbersome?

- Why can't there be an easier way to execute packages via T-SQL, without having to use `xp_cmdshell`?

- Isn't there a more secure way to store sensitive configuration information, such as database passwords?

Fortunately, there were many other data professionals who were asking similar questions, and Microsoft listened. In 2012, we got all these things and more.

Unveiled: The SSIS Catalog

With the release of SQL Server 2012, Microsoft introduced the SSIS catalog as a brand-new way to manage the deployment, storage, and execution of SSIS packages. While the legacy tools for storing and executing packages were still in place, the SSIS catalog was the new path forward.

The SSIS catalog was built to be the center of the universe when it comes to Integration Services packages. It was designed to serve as the deployment target for storing packages, eliminating the need to store packages in the MSDB database. Packages deployed to the SSIS catalog were also executed using built-in logic in catalog stored procedures, allowing for easy execution of packages via T-SQL. It also simplified the logging process, enabling a simple runtime setting to define how packages are logged. Finally, it improved security by allowing more granular controls over who would do what to which packages.

The SSIS catalog addressed several major concerns, but also introduced a few new challenges. ETL developers and architects had to rethink how packages were stored, and how configuration values were used. In the early days, the catalog logging tables had some less-than-optimal indexes, requiring an update from Microsoft to address performance issues. However, despite these few minor shortcomings, the SSIS catalog was a welcome addition and quickly became the de facto standard for storing and executing SSIS packages.

Today, the SSIS catalog is a fourth-generation product, and has matured greatly since it was released. It has evolved well, improving in both performance and usability. In my role as a consultant, I find it very easy to recommend using the SSIS catalog for new or migrated ETL projects.

About This Book

This book was written for data professionals who are (or will be) developing or supporting SQL Server Integration Services projects in the enterprise. I've done my best to compose these chapters so that they can be used as a getting-started guide by those new to the SSIS catalog, and as a reference for those who are already supporting catalog-deployed SSIS projects. It is assumed that the reader has some experience building or supporting SSIS packages.

Companion Website

We have published a companion website at **SSISCatalogBook.com**. This site has the downloadable source code from each of the code examples shown in this book, as well as a listing of each of the external links shared herein. We've also included an errata section to point out any errors or ambiguity in this text after publication.

Chapter 1

Meet the SSIS Catalog

The SSIS catalog brought about a significant shift in the way SSIS packages are stored, executed, and logged. In the coming chapters I'll walk through the moving parts of the SSIS catalog, but let's first start with a brief review of how we got here.

History of SSIS Package Management

When SQL Server Integration Services was introduced in 2005, there were two ways to store your SSIS packages: in SQL Server or on the file system.

Packages could be deployed to an instance of SQL Server, where they would reside within predefined tables in the MSDB database. Packages could also be stored on the file system, which required nothing more than simply copying the packages from the development folder to a user-defined execution folder. There was also a hybrid approach referred to as the Package Store, in which packages would be deployed to a known directory and would then appear in the list of accessible packages within MSDB (even though they were physically stored on the file system).

Once the packages were deployed to either the file system or MSDB, they could be executed manually or through a scheduled process. Packages would be executed using one of the built-in execution utilities - DTExec.exe or DTExecUI.exe – or through the UI in SQL Server Agent. There was no built-in way to execute packages using T-SQL, although a creative solution could be built for this by invoking DTExec.exe using `xp_cmdshell`.

In the pre-2012 versions of SSIS, using the built-in logging tools was cumbersome. One could set packages to log to a destination such as a flat file, XML file, or a SQL Server table in MSDB (my preference), but each package had to be individually configured at design time for such logging, and any modification to that logging required a code change. Further, the log information wasn't very detailed, consisting mostly of informational messages generated during package execution. As spartan as it was, however, the logging tool in older versions of SSIS was certainly better than nothing.

The Catalog Changes Everything

When SQL Server 2012 was released, it introduced the SSIS catalog as a new way to store, execute, and log SSIS packages. Rather than relying on MSDB to manage storage of packages, SSIS instead got its own database. That database and the code surrounding it are collectively referred to as the SSIS catalog, which is designed to be the nucleus of a modern Integration Services ETL architecture.

Among the major changes that were introduced with the SSIS catalog:

- *A separate, dedicated database.* After sharing a database with SQL Server agent jobs, backup logs, and other system-level information, the SSIS catalog brings together all the SSIS-related information in a database dedicated to that purpose. This database, which is named SSISDB, includes storage for the packages as well as logging and configuration information.

- *Built-in logging.* The catalog is built with a rich set of tables for logging most every detail of each execution. The logging process was made much easier by making it a built-in part of the execution rather than a separate operation that had to be configured for each package.

- *Project-centric storage.* Using the SSIS catalog for storage shifts from package-level to project-level storage. Packages are still individually executed and configured, but are deployed to the catalog on a project-by-project basis (with some exceptions to be discussed later).

- *T-SQL interface.* The SSIS catalog encapsulates almost every operation – including management, deployment, execution, and logging – into T-SQL views and stored procedures. No longer does one have to build creative workarounds to execute or otherwise manage SSIS assets! By exposing all of these behaviors through T-SQL, package execution and management is much simpler and easier to automate.

- *Configuration through environments.* The SSIS catalog also introduced the concept of environments. In catalog lingo, an environment is a collection of variables that are passed to a package at runtime. Catalog environments perform a similar function to package configurations, except that environments reside in the catalog database itself and are thus easier to deploy, manage, and secure.

Along with these major developments, there were numerous smaller additions, including a new SSIS management UI in SQL Server Management Studio. I'll explore each of these new features in greater detail later in this book.

Deployment Models

To allow SSIS packages to take full advantage of these new features while still providing legacy support for existing projects, Microsoft introduced the concept of the deployment model in 2012. The deployment model is a project-level setting that defines how that package will be stored and executed.

The selection of a deployment model is made on a project-by-project basis, allowing flexibility for environments with a mix of legacy code and new development.

There are two different options: package deployment model and project deployment model.

Project Deployment Model

The project deployment model is the default setting for any new SSIS project created using SQL Server Data Tools (SSDT). When using project deployment model, all the catalog-related features are available for use in package development and execution.

There were quite a few new Integration Services features that were introduced in the same version that the SSIS catalog made its debut. While this book doesn't exhaustively cover all of those new things, the following is a brief list of behaviors that are related to the SSIS catalog. These features are only available when using the project deployment model.

- *Parameterization.* This is one of my two favorite new features of the project deployment model. The parameterization features allow the SSIS developer to add read-only parameters to packages and/or projects. This works in much the same way that package configurations did, in that parameters can be attached to package properties (connection strings, file paths, and other values) to substitute the runtime value from the parameter for an otherwise static value. Parameters improve upon configurations in that they are clearly exposed to processes that invoke them, unlike configurations that were mostly hidden and very easy to forget. Parameters can be created at the package level or project level, and can be marked as required to force the user or calling process to supply a value. Parameters can also be set to obfuscate sensitive data if that parameter contains information such as passwords.

- *Fully integrated logging.* The second of my two favorite features of the catalog and the project deployment model. The built-in logging that is available when using project deployment model is as close to fully automatic logging as you can get in an ETL process. This book will go much more into detail in a later chapter on the logging facilities in the SSIS catalog.

- *Environments.* To manage groups of parameters, environments can be created to associate a set of input values that will be passed to one or more packages at runtime. Environments are dissociated from individual packages, so they can be managed at the server (catalog) level and applied to packages across multiple projects.

The package deployment model (sometimes referred to as the legacy deployment model) was created to support packages developed in older versions of SSIS. Using the package deployment model, features such as logging, configurations, and deployment behave the same way as they did in SQL Server 2005 and 2008. For new SSIS projects, the default setting is to use project deployment model, so you'll have to manually change this for any new project that you want to set to package deployment model.

As a matter of practice, package deployment model is reserved for older SSIS packages that were migrated from a pre-2012 version of SQL Server. When package deployment model is used, many of the new features mentioned in the prior section (including parameterization and enterprise logging) will not work. Also, projects using the package deployment model may not be deployed to the SSIS catalog, and must be stored in and executed from the file system or MSDB.

While it is important to understand the distinction between the project and package deployment models, this book will focus on the former. Because project deployment mode is required for catalog deployment, the examples and other references used from this point forward will assume the use of the project deployment model.

A New Way to Manage ETL

To be clear, SQL Server Integration Services wasn't broken prior to the arrival of the SSIS catalog. I was building ETL processes using legacy versions of SSIS for at least five years, and I'd wager that some of those processes are still in place, most likely without the benefit of the SSIS catalog.

While I almost always recommend to my clients that they use the SSIS catalog when deploying to modern versions of SQL Server, there are cases in which it might not be the best solution. I recall a case some years back in which a client had made significant time investments creating a custom logging mechanism in SSIS. When they moved these packages to SSIS 2012, they could have deployed to the SSIS catalog and used its built-in logging instead of their custom tools. However, they had tuned their own logging invention over several years, and it worked very well for them. There is a tool for every job, and the SSIS catalog would have required a great deal of rework in this particular case.

Situations like that, however, are the exception. For nearly all new SSIS development projects, and the majority of SSIS project upgrades, the effort to move to the SSIS catalog is overshadowed by the significant benefits it brings.

The SSIS catalog took a good thing and improved upon it. SSIS was already a well-designed and stable means of moving and massaging data, and the catalog made some of those previously manual processes much easier.

Chapter 2

SSIS Catalog Architecture

Those of us who cut our teeth on pre-catalog versions of SSIS (or perhaps even DTS) recall what a challenge it could be to manage an ETL infrastructure on those legacy platforms. Set aside for a moment the complexities inherent in building the actual packages; even after the packages were created and ready to be merged into production, the effort required to set up configurations, execution code, logging, and other necessities could easily surpass the work put into building the ETL logic.

Although the SSIS catalog is not a silver bullet for every ETL management challenge, the architecture certainly takes away some of the major pain points.

Overview

The catalog uses a simpler and more intuitive way of interacting than did its predecessor. The user interface in SQL Server Management Studio is easy to understand even for those with limited SSIS experience. For those more comfortable with scripting rather than UI tasks, the catalog exposes almost all of its behaviors via T-SQL, through views (for browsing) or stored procedures (for manipulating or executing).

From the initial connection, it is obvious that the catalog is a completely different animal. In earlier versions of SSIS, browsing the inventory of packages required a separate connection in SQL Server Management Studio (SSMS). The SSIS catalog simplifies this by exposing the catalog assets in another node in the conventional Object Explorer window in SSMS, as highlighted below.

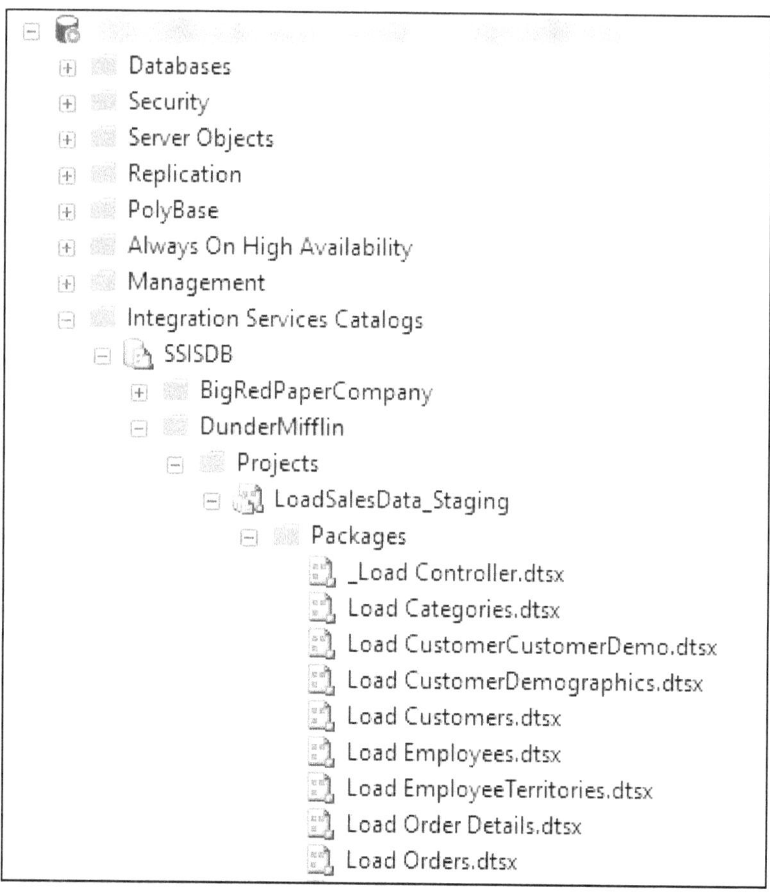

Through this interface in SSMS, we can perform almost any operation against the catalog: deploy projects, execute packages, view execution logs, set security, among many others.

Even though the catalog node on the SSMS interface reads "Integration Services Catalogs" (note the plural), each instance of SQL Server can have a maximum of one SSIS catalog. The catalog, and its underlying database, are always named SSISDB. Each SSIS catalog stands on its own, retaining all the packages and executions logs specific to that catalog.

The SSIS Service

While we're going over architecture, it bears mentioning that there is a Windows service named SSIS Service created during the installation of

SQL Server. This service was designed when packages were still deployed to the MSDB database. In catalog-based SSIS architectures, the functionality of the Windows service is now part of the management layer on top of the SSIS catalog.

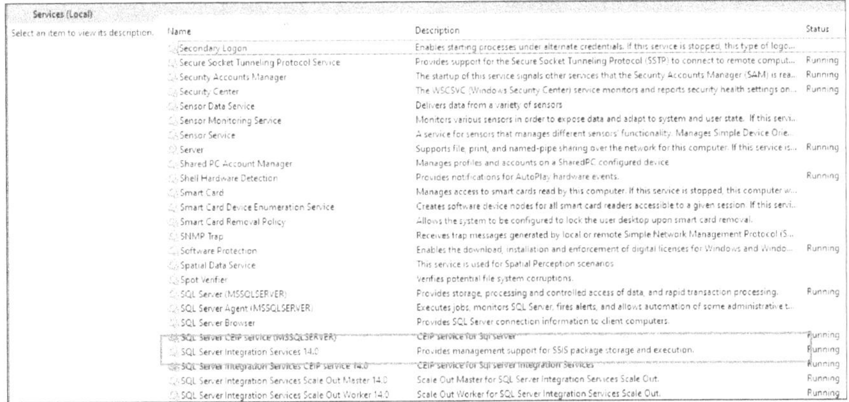

If you are using the SSIS catalog to store and execute SSIS packages, this service is not necessary. In fact, you can disable it entirely on SQL Server database instances that have no packages deployed to the MSDB database or the Package Store.

Creating the Catalog

Even when the SSIS runtime components are selected during the installation of SQL Server, the catalog itself is not automatically created. Creating the SSIS catalog is a relatively simple operation that can be performed in SSMS. Right-clicking on the Integration Services Catalogs node and selecting Create Catalog will bring up the dialog box to create a new SSIS catalog as shown below.

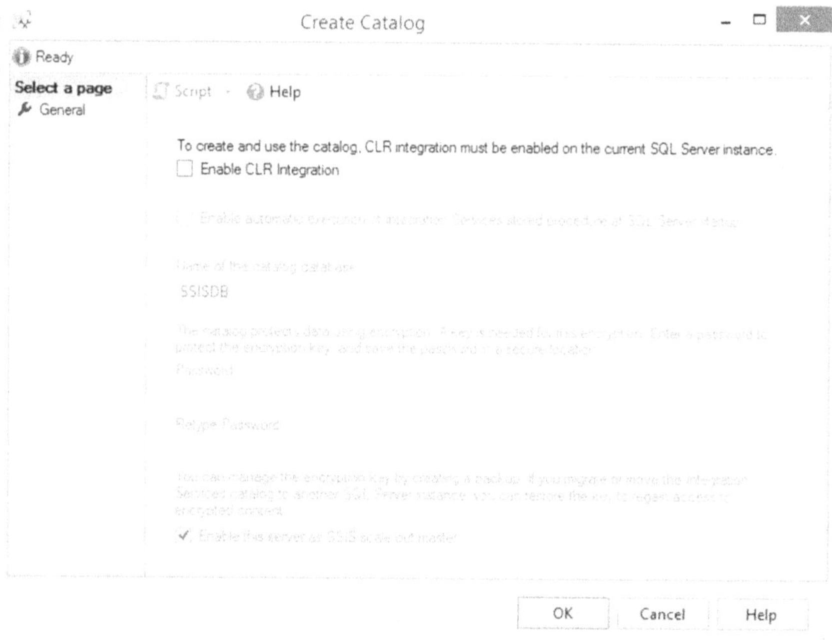

The configuration options presented are these:

- *Enable CLR Integration.* To use the SSIS catalog, the SQL Server Common Language Runtime (CLR) has to be enabled. If the CLR is already enabled, the box will be checked and greyed out (disabled) in this window.

- *Enable automatic execution of Integration Services stored procedures at SQL Server startup.* This optional setting allows the execution of startup procedures for background SSIS processes, such as cleaning up from a failed execution. I haven't found any reason not to enable this, so I always turn it on.

- *Name of the catalog database.* Technically, you don't have an option here – the catalog will always be named SSISDB.

- *Password.* This is the password used to encrypt sensitive values such as stored passwords. Although you won't need to use this password in day-to-day interaction with the SSIS catalog, you'll need to document it in cases of disaster recovery, or if the SSISDB database needs to be restored or moved. Use a secure password, and make sure you securely store it in your password management system.

- *Enable this server as SSIS scale out master.* On SQL Server 2017 or newer, this option is present to configure this catalog server as a scale-out master. Scale-out will be discussed in greater detail in a later chapter.

With these options set, the catalog is ready to be created. After creation, the new SSISDB node will be present beneath the Integration Services Catalogs node in SQL Server Management Studio. The new SSISDB database will also be present in the list of user databases on that instance of SQL Server.

Behind the scenes, the process of creating the SSIS catalog invokes a database restore operation on a SQL Server backup file containing an empty SSISDB database. The reason I know this is that, on a couple of occasions, I found that backup file was missing from the SQL Server installation directory and the catalog creation failed. If that file is missing, more than likely something went wrong during the installation of the SSIS components, and you'll need to rerun SQL Server setup to add the SSIS runtime.

Catalog Configuration

There are a handful of configuration options that can be set at the catalog level once the catalog has been created. The Catalog Properties window, which can be found by right-clicking on the newly created SSISDB catalog node and choosing Properties from the context menu, is shown in the snippet below.

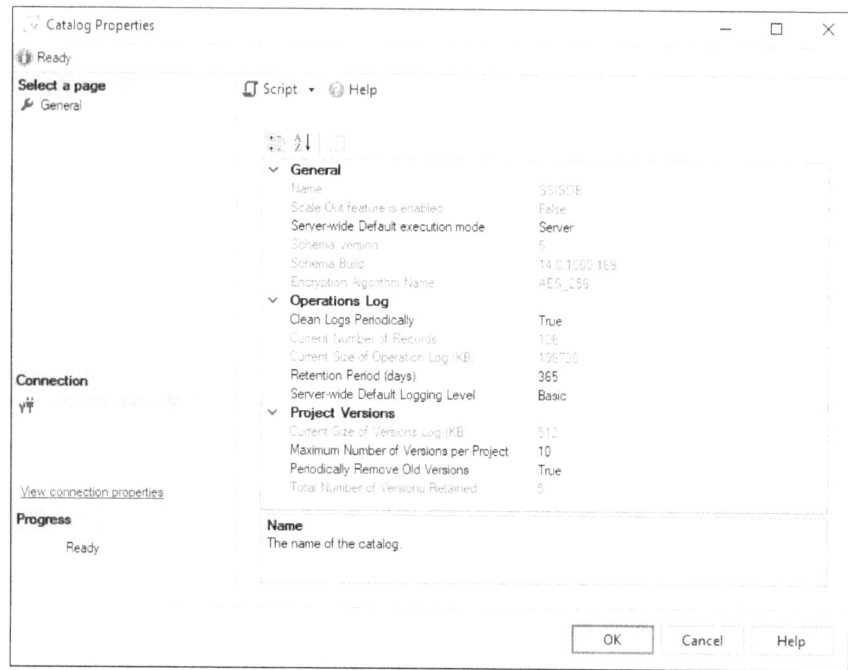

Among the settings that can be configured here:

- *Server-wide Default execution mode*. This is a feature new to SSIS 2017, which allows this catalog instance to be used as a server or a scale-out node. Leave this on Server unless scale-out is enabled and in use on this instance.

- *Clean Logs Periodically*. This setting enables the purge of old records from the SSIS catalog logging tables. The typical setting is to set this to True, meaning that log data will be removed after a certain age (more on that shortly). However, if this option is enabled, make sure that you know the implications of purging SSIS log data! Consider moving the log data to an archive location before purging, to avoid losing that valuable history of execution logs. I'll revisit SSIS log retention later in this book.

- *Retention Period (days)*: If the Clean Logs Periodically setting is set to True, log data older than this setting (in days) will be deleted. The default setting is 365 days, which will keep a rolling 1-year of log data in the SSIS log tables.

- *Server-wide Default Logging Level*. This setting establishes the default value for how logging will be performed. Each package execution can override the runtime setting for logging granularity, but if no value is specified, this default level will be used. The default setting is Basic. We will cover logging levels in more detail in the Execution Logging chapter.

- *Maximum Number of Versions per Project*. This setting defines how many versions of each project will be kept, with a default value of 10. Project versions will be covered in greater depth in the Deployment chapter.

- *Periodically Remove Old Versions*. This setting, which defaults to True, defines whether old versions of projects should be purged.

These settings can also be viewed or set through T-SQL. The catalog view `[catalog].[catalog_properties]` shows these properties, and the stored procedure `[catalog].[configure_catalog]` can be used to update them.

The SSISDB Database

When the SSISDB catalog is created, a matching database named SSISDB will be created on the same SQL Server instance. All of the assets related to the SSIS catalog reside in this database, including the deployed packages, environments, variables, and logging.

From a maintenance perspective, the SSISDB database is just like any other user database on your system. It requires monitoring, regular backups, index maintenance, and related care and feeding.

The internals of the SSISDB database will be covered in depth in a later chapter.

Interacting with the Catalog

The SSIS catalog is exposed as just another node in SQL Server Management Studio when connecting to the host SQL Server instance. Unlike pre-2012 deployments, there is no need to create a separate connection in SSMS to interact with the catalog or the deployed packages it stores.

Most every interaction with the SSIS catalog can be performed using either the UI or through T-SQL. Creating folders, deploying or deleting projects, assigning permissions, configuring catalog settings, and setting up or querying logs can all be done via the user interface or through T-SQL code.

Virtual Folder Structure

The SSIS catalog has an easy-to-understand layout for organizing the deployed projects and environments. These deployed assets are stored in user-defined folders within the SSIS catalog structure. These folders don't physically exist on the file system but are stored as virtual folders within the SSIS catalog tables. When a new folder is created, each one is configured with two virtual subfolders named Projects and Environments in which projects and environments will be stored.

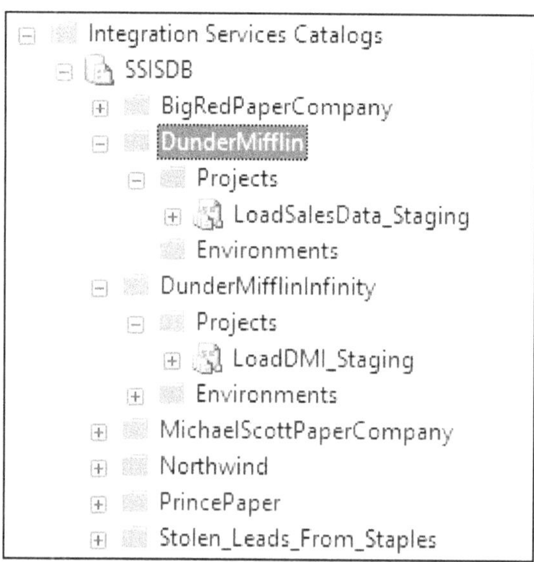

You can create as few or as many user-defined folders here as you wish, but there must be at least one folder beneath SSISDB before any projects or environments can be deployed.

Keep in mind that user-defined folder structure is exactly one level deep. Folders may only be created directly in the SSISDB node of the Integration Services Catalogs hierarchy. Although it would be convenient to create subfolders (specifically, a user-defined folder within another user-defined folder), the catalog only supports one layer of folders.

Deployment

Packages are moved into catalog storage through the deployment process. When a project is deployed to the SSIS catalog, all the code assets for that project are packaged and written to the tables in the SSISDB database.

As with most other operations, deployment can be performed manually through the UI, or through T-SQL scripts. Deployment will be covered in more depth in the Deployment chapter of this book.

Execution

Packages deployed to the SSIS catalog are executed using the catalog interface, which can take on many shapes. As with other catalog-based operations, executions can be invoked through the user interface or programmatically. The SQL Server Agent can also be used to start executions.

There are a lot of variables involved when deciding on an architecture for package execution in the SSIS catalog. This topic is explored in much more detail in the Package Execution chapter.

Execution Reports

The SSIS catalog comes with a handy set of built-in reports that show the execution trends and details for packages executed on that instance of the catalog. These reports are built into SQL Server Management Studio, and show high-level summaries as well as granular details of each execution.

These reports, and logging in general, represent a significant part of the value of using the SSIS catalog. The Execution Logging chapter has much more detail on the execution logging and reporting capabilities of the SSIS catalog.

Deleting the SSIS Catalog

Although it won't be an everyday occurrence, it may be necessary to delete an SSIS catalog from an instance of SQL Server. The most common use for this is to move the SSIS catalog to a different server entirely.

The SSIS catalog can be deleted through one of two ways:

- Delete the catalog from the Integration Services Catalog node in SQL Server Management Studio. This is the preferred method, because this will also delete the SQL Server Agent cleanup jobs associated with the SSIS catalog.

- Drop the underlying SSISDB database. Although this does get rid of the SSIS catalog, this quick-and-dirty method doesn't clean up the SQL Server Agent jobs associated with the catalog.

Catalog Architecture

The design of the SSIS catalog is a significant improvement over the legacy MSDB storage. From the way packages are deployed to and executed from the catalog, to the built-in logging and reporting capabilities, this evolution of SSIS storage and management makes the management of ETL logic much easier than in legacy versions of the product.

Chapter 3
Deployment

Deploying to the SSIS catalog is the means through which the project source code (.dtsx files, project-scoped connection managers, and other assets) are copied from their storage location on the file system into the appropriate tables in the SSISDB database. On the surface, deploying packages to the SSIS catalog looks like a simple operation, but there are several complexities to be aware of when managing package deployments. In addition, there are at least four different tools for handling deployments to the SSIS catalog.

This chapter covers the mechanics of what takes place during a deployment to the SSIS catalog, as well as the tools used for such deployments.

Project-Centric Storage

Before jumping into the methods of deploying to the SSIS catalog, we must first understand deployment granularity. For those using the SSIS catalog for the first time, the concept of project-centric deployment and storage will take a bit of adjustment.

When using a legacy version of SSIS (or a newer version in package deployment mode), the smallest unit of code management was always the package. Those individual DTSX files could be deployed, redeployed, and deleted individually, without regard to or impact to any other packages in that project. There was no hard relationship between packages, with each package standing on its own when stored in the file system or MSDB.

When moving to the SSIS catalog, the granularity of deployment and storage changes. Each SSIS project is treated like an enterprise application, which includes not only packages but project connections and project parameters. Because of this change, the SSIS catalog stores the entire project as one unit rather than storing individual packages. It also means that the deployment process pushes the entire project to the SSIS catalog server at once. Under the hood, the entire project is serialized into a binary value and stored in a table in the SSIS catalog.

How are projects stored in the catalog?

It is possible to work with the SSIS catalog without knowing the details of how packages and projects are physically stored in the SSISDB database. If you work with SSIS long enough, though, at some point you'll need to interrogate the underlying tables directly.

If you explore the SSIS catalog structure, you'll find tables named `[internal].[packages]` and `[internal].[projects]`. Don't be led astray by these object names – the package and project definitions aren't actually stored in either of these tables. These two tables just store some of the metadata around the projects and their contained packages.

The metadata for the projects is actually stored in a table named `[internal].[object_versions]`. Each time a new version of a project is deployed to the catalog, the project definition (along with the packages therein) is stored in the binary `object_data` field in that table.

Do be aware that each project can have multiple versions in the catalog! Project versions will be covered in more depth later in this chapter.

Single-Package Deployment

There can be exceptions to this deployment architecture. In later versions of Integration Services (version 2016 and newer), it is possible to deploy a single package to the SSIS catalog without deploying all of the packages in that project.

When the SSIS catalog was first introduced, Microsoft got a lot of negative feedback from data architects because the all-or-nothing project deployment caused some issues with deployment granularity and source code management. In response to that feedback, the catalog behavior was changed with the release of SQL Server 2016 to allow individual packages to be deployed to the catalog.

This new single-package deployment behavior didn't change the way projects are stored in the catalog. Package-level deployments can target an existing project (which will add the new package or replace it if it already exists) or a new project (in which case it will be treated as a new project deployment with a single package). In the underlying SSISDB database, all of the project assets are serialized and stored as a single value, and that project definition is updated when a single package is deployed.

Even though it is possible to deploy individual packages to the SSIS catalog, I recommend sticking with the project-level deployment. If you deploy a single package to the catalog, it does not attempt to deploy any of the dependent project-level assets such as project connections or project parameters. Therefore, if you create a package that depends on a project-level connection or parameter that was not previously deployed, the package-level deployment will succeed but any execution of that package will fail.

There are some limited cases in which single package deployments are useful, especially in hair-on-fire emergency fix situations. However, for day-to-day code deployment, it's safer and more predictable to deploy the entire project as a single application.

Methods of Deployment

There are several methods to deploying packages to the SSIS catalog. Depending on how your change management and source control system is set up, you may use several – or perhaps all – of these methods at some point.

Each of the methods of deployment performs the same operation behind the scenes. The deployment logic is made available through several tools for maximum flexibility.

The simplest way to deploy projects to the SSIS catalog is to use SQL Server Data Tools. By using the built-in deployment capabilities of SSDT, it is possible to handle package development and deployment in one single session without leaving the development user interface.

To deploy from SSDT, open the Solution Explorer window and right-click on the name of the project. As shown below, the context menu will have the option to Deploy at the top of the list.

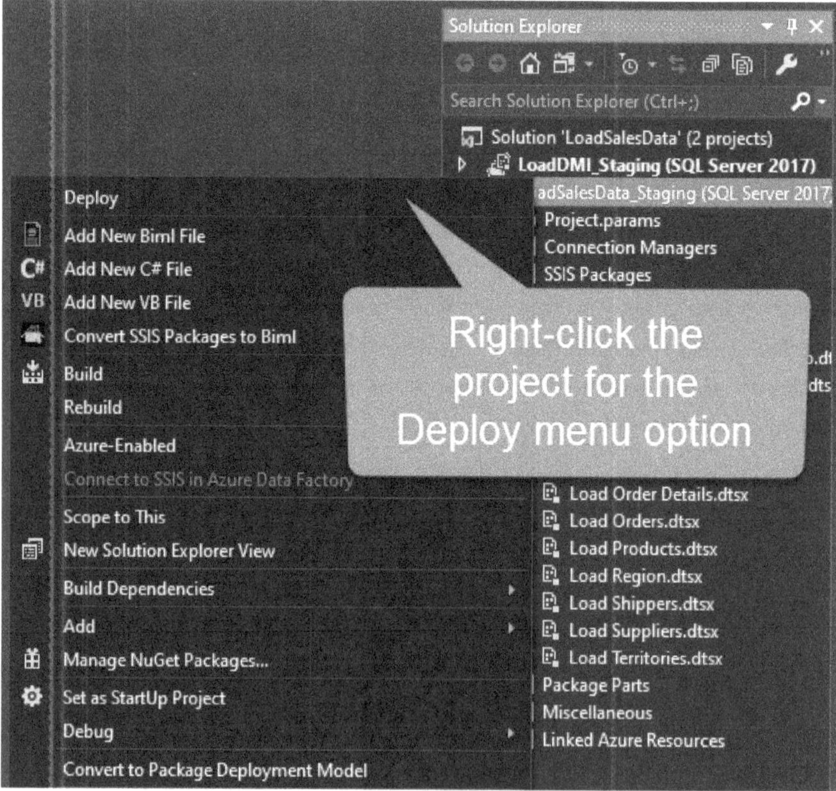

When deploying using this method, a deployment UI will appear, allowing you to select the SQL Server and destination folder to which the project will be deployed.

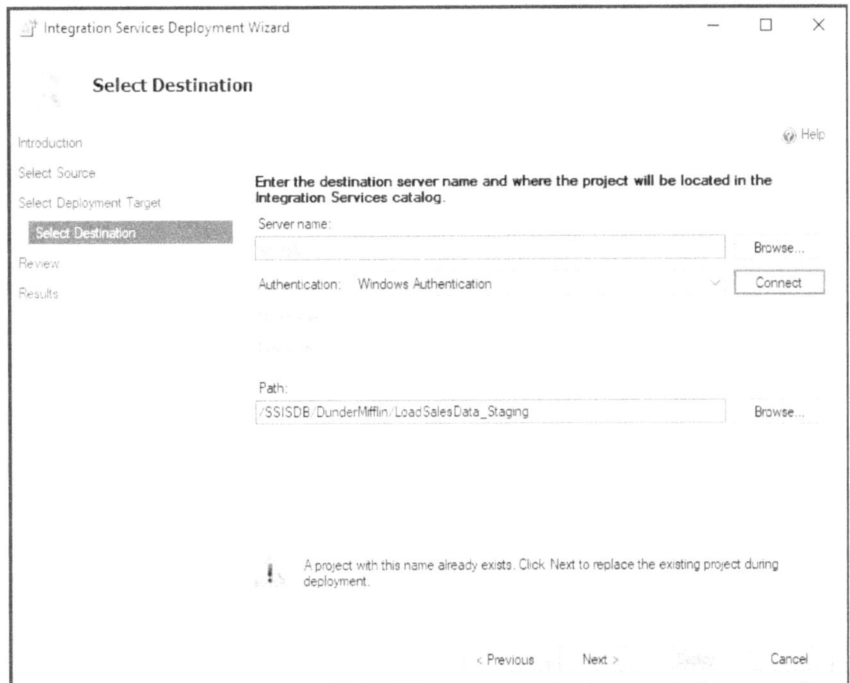

As shown above, the project "remembers" where it was deployed the last time, and reuses those same settings. Also worth noting on the above screenshot is the Authentication setting, which is new to SSDT 2017. In previous versions, one could only connect using Windows authentication when using this deployment method from SSDT (although it is strongly recommended, both for functionality as well as security reasons, to stick with Windows authentication for any SSIS catalog interactions).

Once the deployment target has been set, click through the rest of the deployment wizard (as there are no other settings to specify) and the project will be deployed to the catalog.

This SSDT-based deployment works well in a handful of situations. The most common use is during initial development and testing, in which part of the testing process is to immediately deploy the new or updated SSIS packages to a dev or test catalog server. This method of deployment allows for rapid time-to-test without a lot of barriers between writing code and having a testable version of the project in the SSIS catalog.

This approach does not work as well in organizations that have more rigid change control processes, or in those using continuous integration (CI) for code management and automated testing. Also, since this process of deploying from SQL Server Data Tools is a manual operation, this method has some room for human error such as forgetting to deploy a change or accidentally deploying to the wrong environment (ask me how I know about this one!).

As a final thought on this deployment method, I strongly recommend not using the SSDT deployment to load your project straight into production. Loading a recently-updated project straight from SSDT into a production SSIS catalog bypasses the critical step of testing the updates in a test or user acceptance testing (UAT) version of the catalog. While there are cases in which I have deployed from SSDT straight into production, this is and should be the exception rather than the rule.

Deployment using SQL Server Management Studio UI

Another UI-based approach is to use SQL Server Management Studio to deploy projects to the SSIS catalog. Within the structure of the Integration Services Catalogs nodes is the list of projects, and each of these reveals an option to deploy an existing SSIS project to that folder.

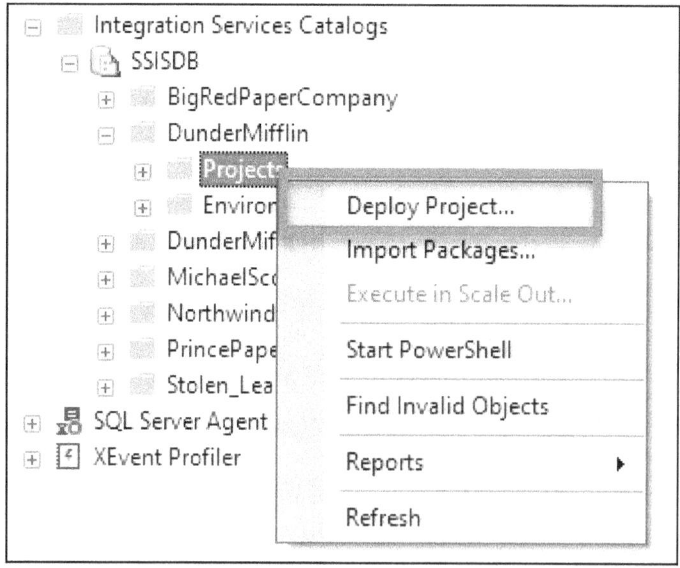

As shown above, using the right-click menu shows the option to deploy a project to the selected folder. Selecting the Deploy Project item opens an SSMS deployment wizard UI to guide you through the process.

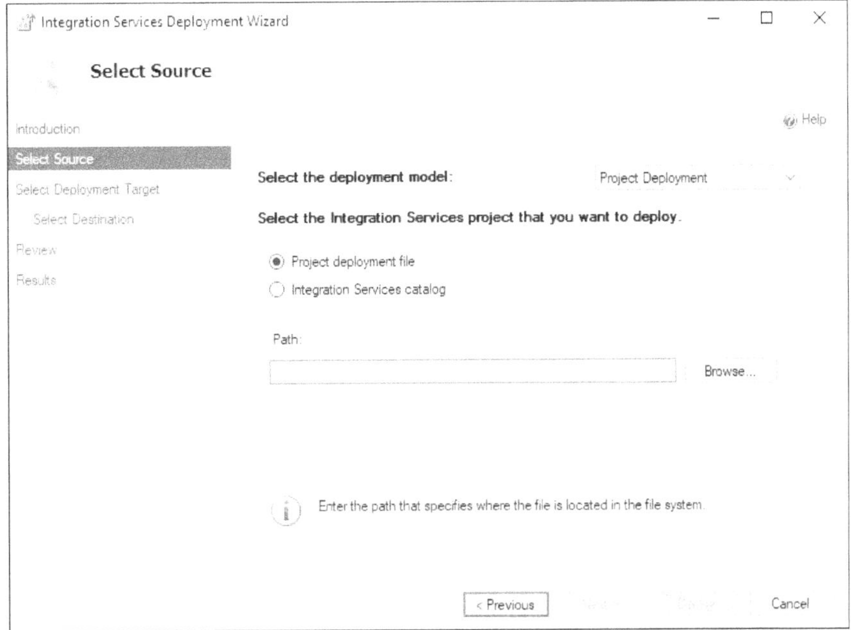

The above wizard prompts for the deployment model (which will always be Project Deployment when pushing to an SSIS catalog) and the location from which the project will be deployed. It is possible to use another SSIS catalog as the source (for example, when manually promoting code from Development to QA), but in most cases, you'll be specifying the location of the SSIS source code on disk. When browsing for the project deployment file, you'll be looking for the .ispac file that corresponds with the project to be deployed.

After selecting the correct .ispac file, you'll be able to specify the catalog and folder to which the project will be deployed (the default values for which will be the catalog and folder where you originally kicked off the Deploy Project wizard). Simply selecting the defaults will deploy to the selected folder in just two additional clicks.

What exactly is an .ispac file?

When working with the SSIS catalog, you'll come across a lot of references to .ispac files. These system-generated files are created during the build in SQL Server Data Tools or from within an automated build process. The .ispac file is really just a zipped copy of all of the project assets (packages, connections, and parameters) formatted so it can be imported into the SSIS catalog. It is the .ispac file that is used as a source for any SSIS catalog deployment.

The .ispac file is automatically created when you perform a build in SSDT. If you are manually deploying packages using the wizard in SSMS or through T-SQL, be sure that you create the .ispac file by invoking a project build through the Build menu in SSDT.

The project's .ispac file can be found in the `bin\<environment>` directory of the SSIS project. If you're ever curious as to the contents of the .ispac file, make a copy of the file and change the extension from .ispac to .zip, and open up that new copy using Windows file explorer. As you'll see, all of your project assets are contained in that file.

This manual deployment process is one of the lesser common means of moving SSIS code into the catalog. Because it is a UI wizard, it requires user intervention to invoke, and suffers from some of the same potential for human error (forgetting to deploy, deploying to the wrong folder, etc.). However, for quick deployment during development and testing, or for organizations without formal code promotion processes, this method can be useful.

Deployment using ISDeploymentWizard.exe

The wizard-driven approach used by both SSDT and SSMS rely on the ISDeploymentWizard.exe application. This app can be invoked directly outside of either SSDT or SSMS by calling **ISDeploymentWizard.exe**, which is typically located in the **C:\Program Files (x86)\Microsoft SQL Server\<Version Number>\DTS\Binn** directory.

When working with the SSIS catalog, you'll find that most everything you can do through the UI in SQL Server Management Studio can also be done via T-SQL. That is certainly the case for deployments. Deploying a new or updated project, creating folder, and even setting up environments (to be discussed in more detail in the next chapter) are all possible through T-SQL stored procedures in the SSIS catalog.

For those who are new to the SSIS catalog, it makes a lot of sense to use the UI to get familiar with deployments and related tasks. However, those UI operations are intended primarily as one-off, manual tasks. Most mature enterprise SSIS architectures use some form of deployment automation, often using T-SQL. Whether or not you expect to use it immediately, you should familiarize yourself with scriptable deployment operations in the SSIS catalog.

The individual tasks that go into package deployment operations are all encapsulated into built-in stored procedures in the SSIS catalog. Below I've listed and briefly described each of the most essential stored procedures you may need for automated package deployments.

`[catalog].[create_folder]`

As noted earlier, all projects must be deployed into a user-defined folder, so creating said folder will be our first step in a new deployment. For automated deployments, it is a good idea to ensure that the target folder already exists, and only try to create it if it doesn't.

As shown below, you can query the `[catalog].[folders]` view to see if the target folder already exists. To create the folder, use the `[catalog].[create_folder]` stored procedure, which expects only the folder name as an input.

```
USE [SSISDB]
GO

-- Check for existing folder
IF NOT EXISTS (
      SELECT 1
      FROM [catalog].[folders]
```

```
        WHERE name = N'DunderMifflin'
)
BEGIN
      -- Create if not present
      EXEC [catalog].[create_folder] N'DunderMifflin'
END
GO
```

There are also stored procedures for renaming ([catalog].[rename_folder]) and deleting ([catalog].[delete_folder]) user-defined folders in the catalog if necessary.

[catalog].[deploy_project]

This stored procedure deploys a project to the SSIS catalog. It takes as inputs the target folder name, target project name, and the binary value of the project being deployed. There is an output parameter that returns an integer value to indicate success (0) or failure (1).

For catalog deployment operations, this will be the most commonly used stored procedure. This stored procedure is used for first-time deployments of a project as well as updates (overwrites) to the same project after the initial deployment.

An example of the use of [catalog].[deploy_project] is shown below.

```
USE [SSISDB]
GO

-- Set  up runtime values
DECLARE @return_val INT
DECLARE @folder_name NVARCHAR(128) = N'DunderMifflin'
DECLARE @project_name NVARCHAR(128) = N'Test Project 1'
DECLARE @project_stream VARBINARY(MAX) = (
      SELECT *
      FROM OPENROWSET(BULK
         'E:\proj1\bin\Development\Test Project 1.ispac'
            , SINGLE_BLOB)
      AS BinaryData
)

DECLARE @operation_id BIGINT
```

```
EXECUTE @return_val = [catalog].[deploy_project]
    @folder_name
        , @project_name
        , @project_stream
        , @operation_id OUTPUT

SELECT @return_val    -- 0 indicates success, 1 means failure

GO
```

As shown, the stored procedure accepts the parameters for the folder, project, and the contents of the .ispac file. You can use this same syntax to deploy a new project or overwrite an existing project with the specified name.

If for some reason you need to programmatically delete a project, you can use the stored procedure `[catalog].[delete_project]`. However, if you are just deploying an updated version of an existing project, there is no need to delete – just call the deployment logic as shown above, and it will replace the old version with the one you specify.

Programmatic Deployment Using PowerShell

For those who prefer automation via PowerShell, there is an SSIS API that can be used to deploy projects to the SSIS catalog. This same API can be used to create folders as well. There is an excellent quick-start document on using PowerShell to deploy projects to the SSIS catalog linked here: **TimMitchell.net/go/psh-catalog-deploy**.

Note that it is also possible to deploy directly via C# if you want to roll your own deployment as part of a larger app dev initiative. Since this uses the same libraries that are used in the PowerShell deployment, the capabilities would be similar to those described in the linked document above.

Project Versioning

Earlier I briefly mentioned the versioning settings in the SSIS catalog properties. The SSIS catalog is equipped with an archive that will keep a small number of previously deployed project versions.

Here's how it works: When a new version of a project is deployed to the SSIS catalog, the .ispac file is serialized into binary and written to the `[internal].[object_versions]` table. If the project being deployed already exists in the target folder in the SSIS catalog, the deployment doesn't overwrite the version currently in the catalog. Rather, the older version remains in that table, with the newly deployed project code having been marked as the effective version. The SSIS catalog will retain a set number of versions per project; by default, a maximum of ten versions of each project will be kept in `[internal].[object_versions]`. You can change the number of versions that are retained for each project using the catalog properties window.

Prior project versions stored in the SSIS catalog are simply there for archival purposes. Regardless of how many old versions of a project are stored in the catalog, only one of them is marked as the active version. When executing one or more packages or exporting the project to an .ispac file, the logic in the active version is the one used for these operations.

By default, the most recently deployed version of any project is the one marked as active. During the deployment process, the newly deployed version will be marked as the current version, thus demoting the currently active version to an archive.

You can view all the versions of any given project from the Object Explorer in SQL Server Management Studio. When you right-click on a project in the Integration Services Catalogs node, the `Versions…` context menu item will take you to a list of versions of that project stored in the catalog.

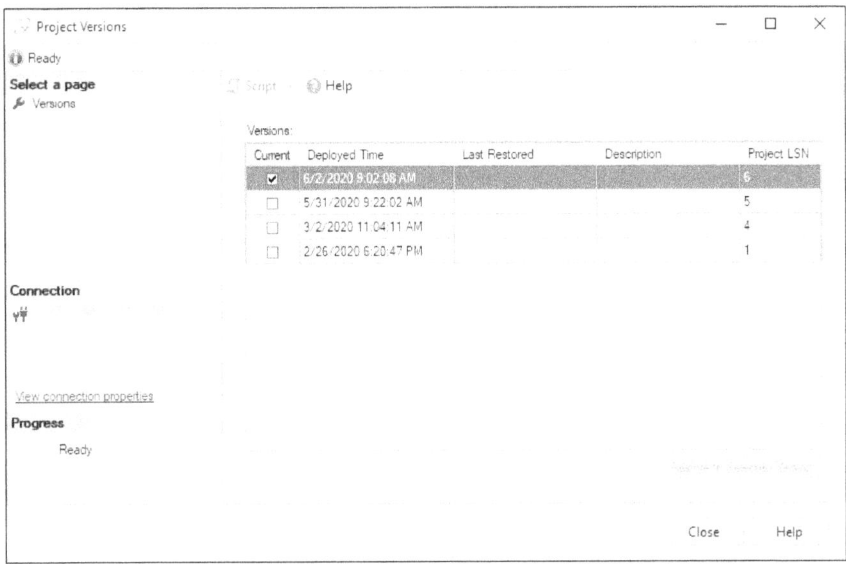

As shown, the details of current and prior versions for a single project is displayed in the Project Versions window. It is important to note that this may not be the full history of deployed code for that project. Because the catalog will only store a specific number of versions for each project, older versions will disappear to stay within that set number of versions.

Using this same Project Versions window, you can quickly restore a prior version of a project to the currently active version by selecting the version you want to restore and clicking Restore to Selected Version. When an older version is restored, It doesn't really "restore" anything. The selected version is simply marked as active, but all other versions of the project will still be retained in the SSIS catalog.

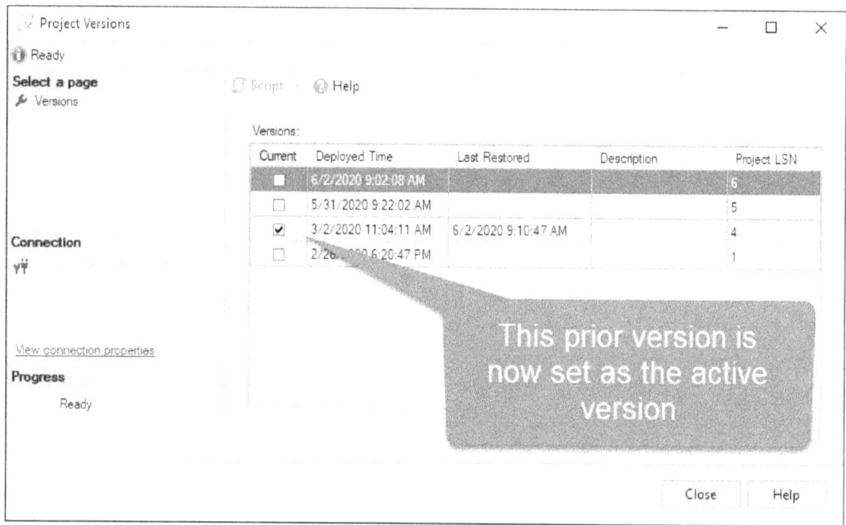

After restoring an older version of the code, that prior version will now be used when executing any package in the specified project.

How should one use project versions?

When I demonstrate to clients and class attendees the versioning functionality of SSIS, a common question that comes up is, "How and when do we use this?"

The project versioning feature in the SSIS catalog is a useful tool, but it's probably not one you'll need for everyday ETL work. There are two specific scenarios that come to mind where the project versioning capability will come in handy.

Recovering from an accidental deployment. The first use case for versioning is what I refer to as the "Oops Moment": the sudden realization that you've prematurely deployed code to the catalog, or perhaps accidentally pushed it to Production when you meant to send it for testing. In such a case, there is no need to go back and retrieve the code from source control; simply open the Project Versions window and set the older version as the active version.

Regression testing. The second use case for project versioning is regression testing. If you discover issues in a newly deployed version of the project code, you can easily revert back to a known-good version for quick regression testing. You can even set the active version programmatically by writing directly to the underlying SSIS catalog tables, though I doubt if this is officially supported by Microsoft.

Under the hood, the project versions are stored in the `internal.object_versions` table. To find which of these versions is the active version for each project, you can query the `object_version_lsn` field in the `internal.projects` table, which indicates the version number currently marked as active for each project in the catalog.

Project Versioning Is Not Source Control!

Keep in mind that the project versioning capability in the SSIS catalog is not a substitute for proper source control. While this feature has some usefulness, it lacks essential features such as branching, merging, and release management found in a true source control system.

Chapter 4

Package Execution

Now that we've reviewed the essentials of the SSIS catalog and how packages are deployed to and stored there, let's talk about where the real work of data integration is done: the execution of a deployed SSIS package.

What is a Package Execution?

A *package execution* is the invocation of the ETL logic built into a single package file. When an SSIS package is executed, the XML hidden in each .dtsx file is translated in memory into logical objects, including connections, tasks, variables, and data flow elements.

A package may be executed in one of several different ways. The most visible way to execute an SSIS package is to invoke it from the SQL Server Data Tools designer. This is the most common way to run functional tests on a package still in development; it is very easy to kick off a package execution and see a visual representation of what is happening, providing quick insight into the details of the execution. While useful for testing and debugging, executing SSIS packages from SSDT has a lot of limitations, the most critical of which is the fact that these interactive executions cannot be scheduled – it is a fully manual process.

Package Execution in the SSIS Catalog

When a package stored in the SSIS catalog is executed, the SQL Server on which the SSIS catalog resides will handle the orchestration of starting the package, logging its output, and recording its progress and final status. If any data flow tasks are in use on the package, the physical memory on the server hosting the SSIS catalog will be used to temporarily store the in-flight data as it passes through the data flow transformations.

There are several different ways to start packages stored in the SSIS catalog. Each of these methods is listed below.

Package Execution via SQL Server Agent

Using SQL Server agent is the most common way to manage recurring SSIS package executions. SQL Server Agent is a mature and capable scheduling tool, and is available in every commercial version of SQL Server. SQL Server Agent has built-in support for executing catalog-deployed SSIS package, with a user interface that is reasonably easy to navigate.

Adding a SQL Server Agent job to invoke a package stored in the SSIS catalog requires three major tasks:

- **Create the job in SQL Server Agent**. A SQL Server Agent job is basically a container for one or more steps, the job alone doesn't actually invoke the package – that work is done in a job step described below.

- **Create a job step to execute the SSIS package**. Once the SQL Server Agent job is created, you can add job steps (tasks) to that job. The job step is the component that actually kicks off the SSIS package. You can have more than one job step per job, and they need not all be the same type (for example, a single job can contain a mix of T-SQL and SSIS package execution job steps).

- **Set up the schedule (optional)**. If you want this job to run automatically on a scheduled basis, you'll need to set up the schedule on which it will run.

When you create the job step to invoke the SSIS package from the catalog, you'll be greeted with an interface similar to the one shown below. Setting the Type property of the Job Step will prompt you for the name of the SQL Server instance on which the SSIS catalog resides, as well as the path of the package to execute.

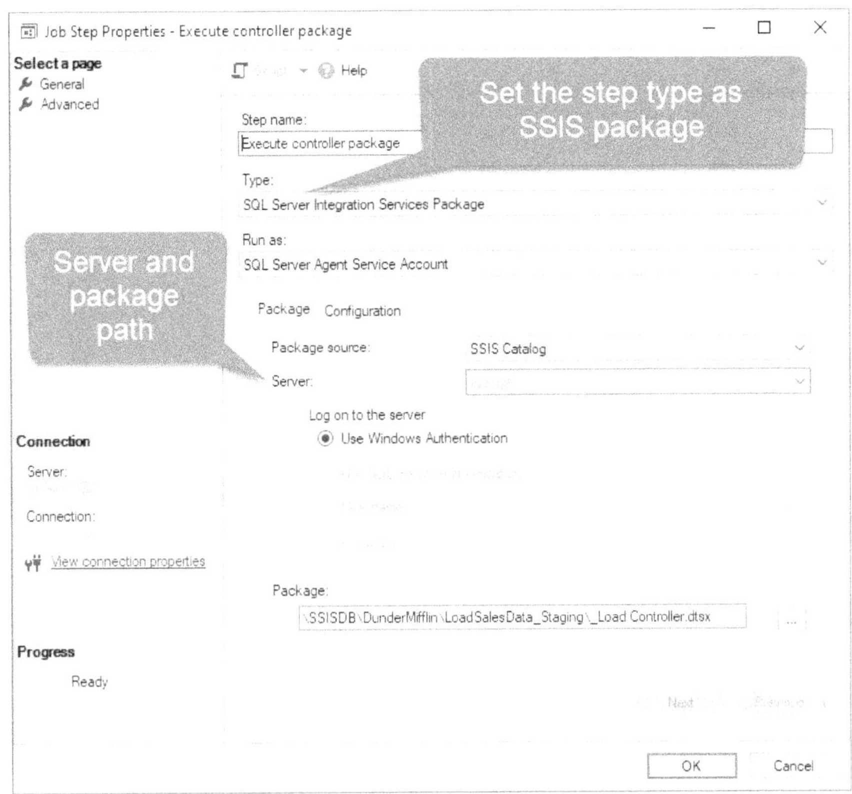

Once the package location has been set, use the Configuration tab to set other package execution options. Clicking on the Configuration tab shows a sub-menu with three more tabs; the first of these allows you to set execution parameter values as shown below.

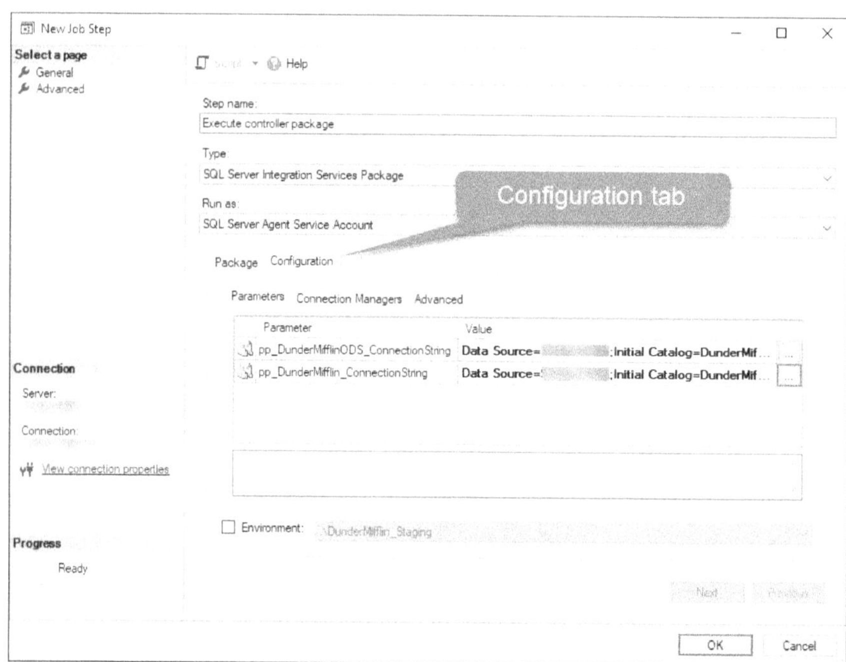

Note that the parameters for this project already have values specified. When you deploy the SSIS package, it will write to a catalog table (specifically, `internal.object_parameters`) the values for any package or project parameters that are not marked either sensitive or required. When executing a package, these default parameter values will be used unless you supply replacement values for them.

You may also notice the Environment setting near the bottom of this page. If you have one or more SSIS catalog environments set up (more on this topic later in this chapter), you would be able to select the environment to use for this job step.

The second tab, Connection Managers, allows you to set properties of each connection manager in that package or its parent project. I'm only going to show this for illustration purposes, as I recommend avoiding this method for setting connection manager properties. Setting up and using parameters for connection string properties is a more maintainable solution.

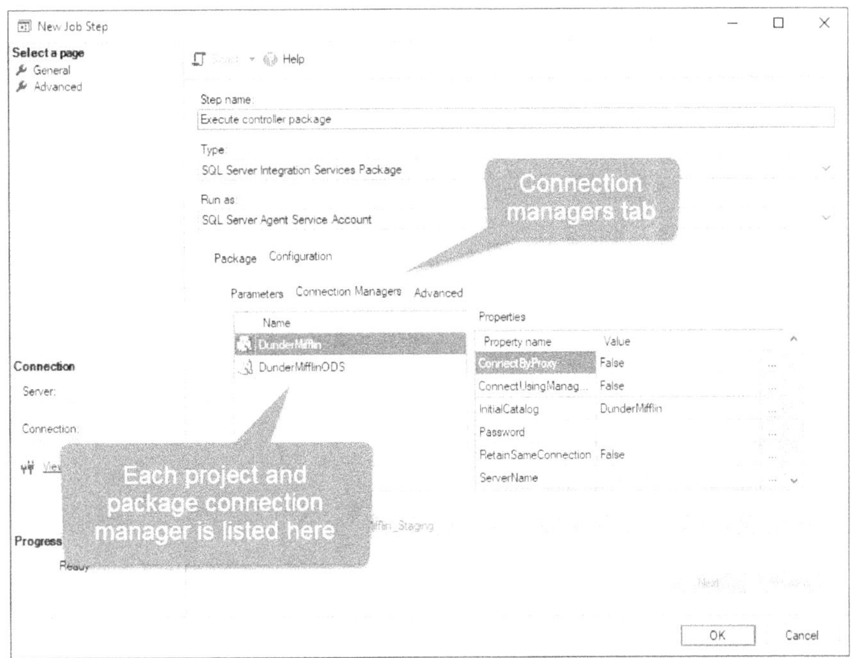

The last of these SSIS job step configuration pages is the Advanced tab. Here you will specify the logging level (covered in greater detail later in this book), whether to use the 32-bit runtime, and any manual property overrides.

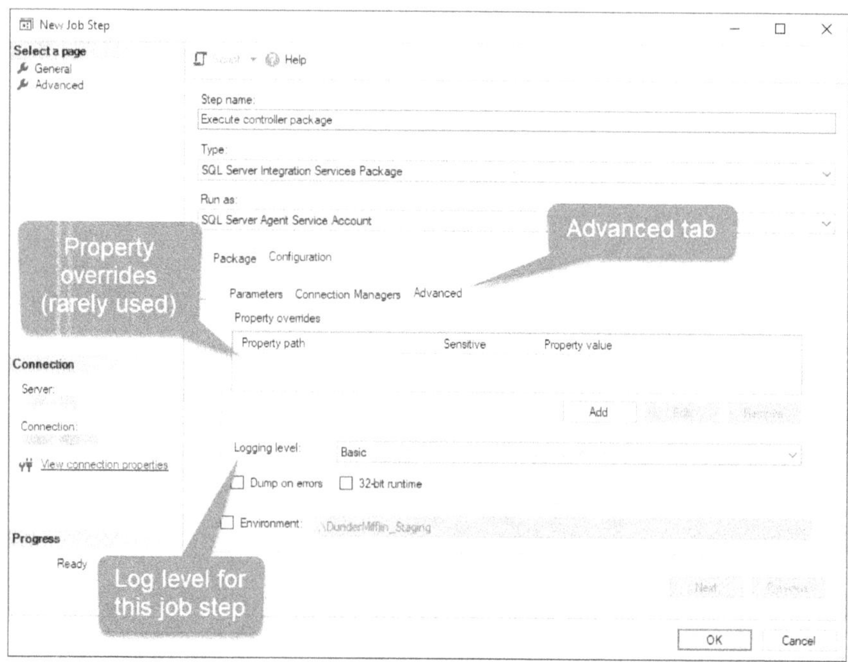

It is important to note that all these settings – parameter values, environment, logging levels, etc. – are all being set only for this single job step. Setting those values does not change the configuration of the package in the catalog, and will not impact any other manual or scheduled package executions.

Unless your organization is already using a commercial enterprise scheduling tool, I highly recommend using SQL Server Agent as the execution mechanism for SQL Server. Most projects I work on use SQL Server Agent as the scheduling engine for SSIS packages; it is versatile, easy to use, and is already installed on the SQL Server running the SSIS catalog.

Package Execution in SQL Server Management Studio

Executing a catalog-deployed package using SQL Server Management Studio is one of the easiest ways to kick off an SSIS package. To begin an execution like this, navigate to the Integration Services Catalogs node of the SQL Server and drill down to the package you wish to execute. Right-clicking the package will bring up the option to Execute, among other items.

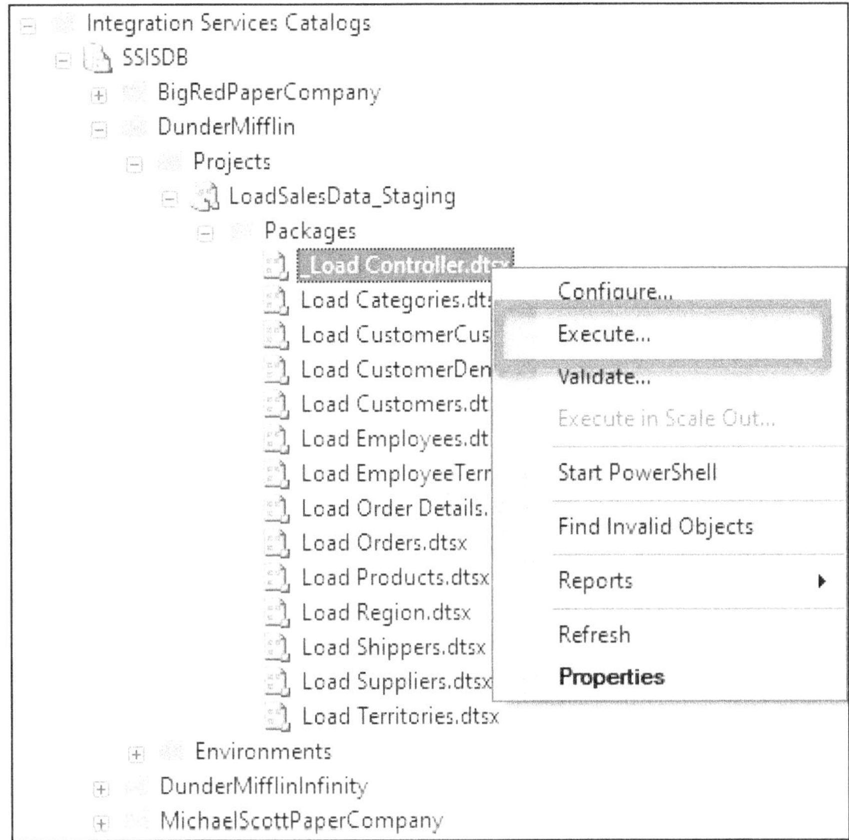

When you choose Execute from this context menu, the Execute Package dialog box will appear.

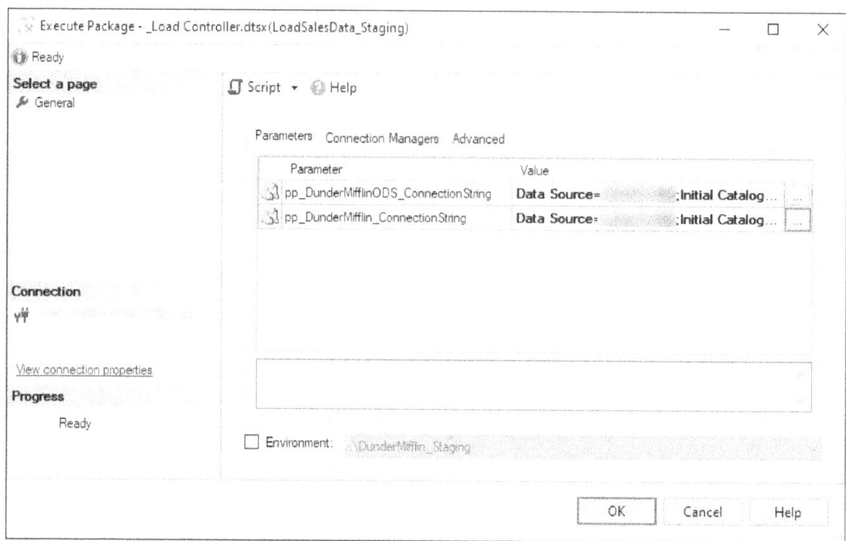

You'll probably notice that this looks very similar to the Job Step Properties window for configuring an SSIS package. In fact, the execution configuration options in the Execute Package window – including parameters, environment specifications, connection manager overrides, and logging level – are identical to those in the job step setup. The only functional difference is that the options set in the Execute Package dialog shown here only apply to the current execution, while those same options saved in a SQL Server Agent job step would be stored for future executions of that same job step.

Once you have configured all the execution options, click OK to start the execution. This will run the package on the SSIS catalog server. When the package starts, you will be presented with a dialog box similar to the following.

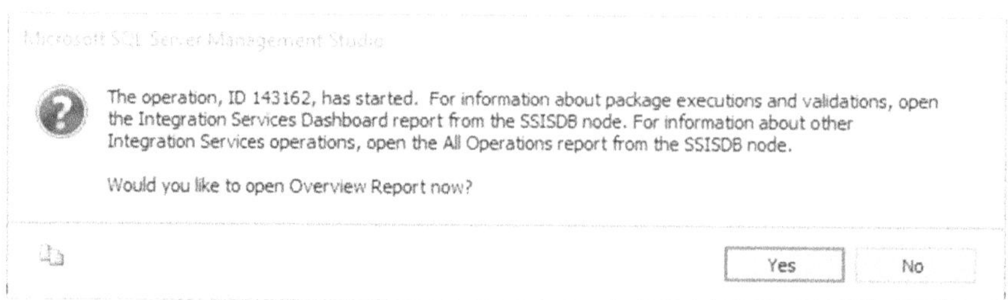

As shown, this feedback confirms that the package execution has commenced, and you are prompted as to whether you wish to open the Overview Report. This report (and other built-in reports) will be covered in greater detail in the next chapter.

Another way to execute an SSIS package is to invoke it from another package – in effect, packages executing other packages. This is a very common design pattern, commonly referred to as a parent-child architecture. If a package is built *solely* for the purpose of invoking other packages, we usually call that an orchestrator or controller package. If you haven't used this parent-child process design pattern before, I would suggest reading through my blog post on ETL atomicity (**TimMitchell.net/etl-atomicity/**) that lays out some of the reasons to break apart ETL logic into smaller packages which can then be invoked by an orchestrator parent package.

To invoke a package from another package, the most common method is to use the Execute Package Task. This task allows you to execute another package in the current project, a package stored in the MSDB database, or one that resides on the file system.

> ***Why won't the Execute Package Task invoke a package in another project stored in the SSIS catalog?***
>
> That's a great question, and I wish I had a good answer to this. The short answer is that you can still execute a package in another project stored in the SSIS catalog, but you'll have to use the Execute SQL Task to invoke the package via T-SQL.

I will circle back briefly on this topic when we discuss logging in the next chapter, since this packages-executing-packages design pattern can have implications on how activity is written to the SSIS logging tables.

One of the most practical improvements added to the SSIS catalog is the ability to execute packages directly via T-SQL. By simply calling a few stored procedures, you can easily create a new execution, add parameters, and then start the execution of that package.

Starting package executions from T-SQL requires that you have some understanding of how a package execution works under the hood. For any package execution in the SSIS catalog – regardless of execution method – the following steps will take place:

- An execution record is inserted into the `[internal].[executions]` table. Think of this as a placeholder for an execution that has not yet started.

- Optional runtime elements can be added to the execution. Here you can apply parameters and set up data taps for this execution.

- Start the execution. It is at this point that the package goes through its full execution routine, starting with validating metadata and concluding with any logging.

When executing a package through the SSMS UI, the details of this multi-step process are mostly hidden from you. When invoking a package from T-SQL, though, you'll have to code each of these steps, which requires a bit more work but also offers greater flexibility.

Shown below is an ordinary package execution invoked via T-SQL.

```
-- Step 1: Create the execution
DECLARE @x_id BIGINT;

EXEC [catalog].[create_execution]
     @package_name = N'_Load Controller.dtsx'
    , @execution_id = @x_id OUTPUT
    , @folder_name = N'DunderMifflin'
    , @project_name = N'LoadSalesData_Staging'
    , @use32bitruntime = False
    , @reference_id = NULL
    , @runinscaleout = False
```

```sql
-- Step 2: Configure to add parameters
EXEC [catalog].[set_execution_parameter_value]
      @execution_id = @x_id
    , @object_type = 20
    , @parameter_name = N'pp_SalesODS_ConnectionString'
    , @parameter_value = N'Data Source=.;Initial
Catalog=DunderMifflinODS;provider=SQLNCLI11.1;integrated
security=SSPI;'

EXEC [catalog].[set_execution_parameter_value]
    @execution_id = @x_id
    , @object_type = 20
    , @parameter_name = N'pp_Sales_ConnectionString'
    , @parameter_value = N'Data Source=.;Initial
Catalog=DunderMifflin;Provider=SQLNCLI11.1;Integrated
Security=SSPI;';


-- Step 3: Execute
EXEC [catalog].[start_execution] @execution_id = @x_id
```

The above script will create the execution (Step 1), set values for the parameters (Step 2), and finally start the execution of the package (Step 3).

Do I have to remember the syntax for these steps?

Fortunately, no. You can generate the commands to create, configure, and start an execution by using the UI to execute a package directly from the SSIS catalog as described earlier in this chapter. Instead of clicking the OK button to start the execution, click the Script button toward the upper middle-left of that window, and the UI will create a T-SQL script similar to the above example with the execution options you specified in that window.

One important thing to note about `[catalog].[start_execution]` is that it runs as an asynchronous process by default. This means that when you call `[catalog].[start_execution]`, it will start the package in question and will return immediately, even while the package is still running. This procedure does not wait for the package to finish its execution, nor does it report whether the called package has succeeded or failed. If you have specified a valid and accessible package and have satisfied all of the prerequisites (such as required parameters), the call to the `[catalog].[start_execution]` procedure will return as successful – even if the package fails. While I expect that this is working as designed, I don't love the fact that it works this way. As part of a normal workflow, I would expect that the code to invoke the package execution would wait for that execution to complete, and then report on the success or failure of that execution.

Fortunately, it's fairly easy to force the package execution to work that way. To do so, I typically make two modifications to the example code above:

- I add a SYNCHRONIZED system parameter to the execution, which will force `[catalog].[start_execution]` to run for the entire duration of the package it invokes. The system parameter syntax looks just like that for a user-defined parameter, except that the `@object_type` for a system parameter is 50 (as opposed to 20 for a project parameter or 30 for a package parameter).

- After the package finishes executing, I query `[catalog].[executions]` to check the status of that execution, and then either succeed or fail the batch based on whether the package succeeded.

As shown below, the modifications to wait for completion and report on package failure add a few lines of code to the script, but that extra bit of code makes this routine far more useful.

```sql
-- Step 1: Create the execution
DECLARE @x_id BIGINT;

EXEC [catalog].[create_execution]
        @package_name = N'_Load Controller.dtsx'
        , @execution_id = @x_id OUTPUT
        , @folder_name = N'DunderMifflin'
        , @project_name = N'LoadSalesData_Staging'
```

```sql
        , @use32bitruntime = False
        , @reference_id = NULL
        , @runinscaleout = False


-- Step 2: Configure to add parameters
EXEC [catalog].[set_execution_parameter_value]
        @execution_id = @x_id
        , @object_type = 20
        , @parameter_name = N'pp_SalesODS_ConnectionString'
        , @parameter_value = N'Data Source=.;Initial
Catalog=DunderMifflinODS;provider=SQLNCLI11.1;integrated
security=SSPI;'

EXEC [catalog].[set_execution_parameter_value]
        @execution_id = @x_id
        , @object_type = 20
        , @parameter_name = N'pp_Sales_ConnectionString'
        , @parameter_value = N'Data Source=.;Initial
Catalog=DunderMifflin;Provider=SQLNCLI11.1;Integrated
Security=SSPI;';


-- Step 3: Set the Synchronized property
EXEC [catalog].[set_execution_parameter_value]
        @execution_id = @x_id
        , @object_type = 50
        , @parameter_name = N'SYNCHRONIZED'
        , @parameter_value = 1


-- Step 4: Start the package execution
EXEC [catalog].[start_execution] @execution_id = @x_id


-- Step 5: Retrieve the status of this execution, and fail
--      the batch if the status is anything other than 7
(success)
IF (SELECT status
        FROM catalog.executions
        WHERE execution_id = @x_id) <> 7
RAISERROR('The package has failed. See the error log for
details.'
        , 16
        , 1)
```

As shown above, the additional steps will force the execution to run synchronously (Step 3) and then force a failure if the package was not successful (Step 5).

The ability to invoke catalog-deployed SSIS packages opens up a number of possibilities when it comes to scheduling and other batch operations. In pre-2012 versions of SSIS, the `dtexec.exe` command was the default means for executing an SSIS package. If you were executing a package from a batch of T-SQL operations, you would have had to run the system stored procedure `xp_cmdshell` to call `dtexec.exe`, which is both complicated and risky. Calling a package from a built-in catalog stored procedure simplifies and standardizes this process, and eliminates the risk of enabling `xp_cmdshell`.

Package Execution via dtexec.exe

One of the artifacts carried over from older versions of SSIS is the `dtexec.exe` utility. This lightweight tool can invoke packages stored on the file system, in the msdb database, or in the SSIS catalog. This utility is handy when you have batch processes (which may include PowerShell, Windows batch files, or third-party tools) that need to invoke SSIS packages through a script.

As shown below, the call to `dtexec.exe` uses the `/ISSERVER` directive to indicate that this is a call to an SSIS catalog-deployed package, followed by the full path to the package, and finally the name of the server hosting the package.

```
dtexec.exe /ISSERVER
"\SSISDB\<folder>\<project>\<package>" /SERVER
"<server>"
```

There are also options in `dtexec.exe` that allow you pass in parameters, environment references, and other runtime settings.

The most common use of dtexec.exe is when packages are invoked from third-party applications. If you are executing from SQL Server Agent or another tool that can easily execute T-SQL, it is more straightforward to just use T-SQL to invoke the package.

During development, it is common to execute packages directly from SSDT (or BIDS, if you are using an old version of SSIS). In fact, this is likely the first way you learned to execute an SSIS package. Manually starting a package from SSDT is the simplest and most efficient way to begin testing of a new or newly-modified SSIS package.

It is important to remember that a package invoked from SSDT does not interact with the SSIS catalog. When you start the package from SQL Server Data Tools, the package execution takes place on the machine where SSDT is running, and none of the catalog assets (environment variables, logging tables, etc.) are used. There's nothing wrong with executing like this, especially during testing and development, but be aware that a package execution from SSDT is not a catalog execution.

However, many of the catalog behaviors are still available when executing from SSDT, albeit in a different way. Parameters are still usable, but must be set manually (or left to use the default values). Packages may still invoke other packages using the Execute Package Task. And some of the logging detail is still available for viewing in the Progress tab (shown below) or the Output window of the executing package.

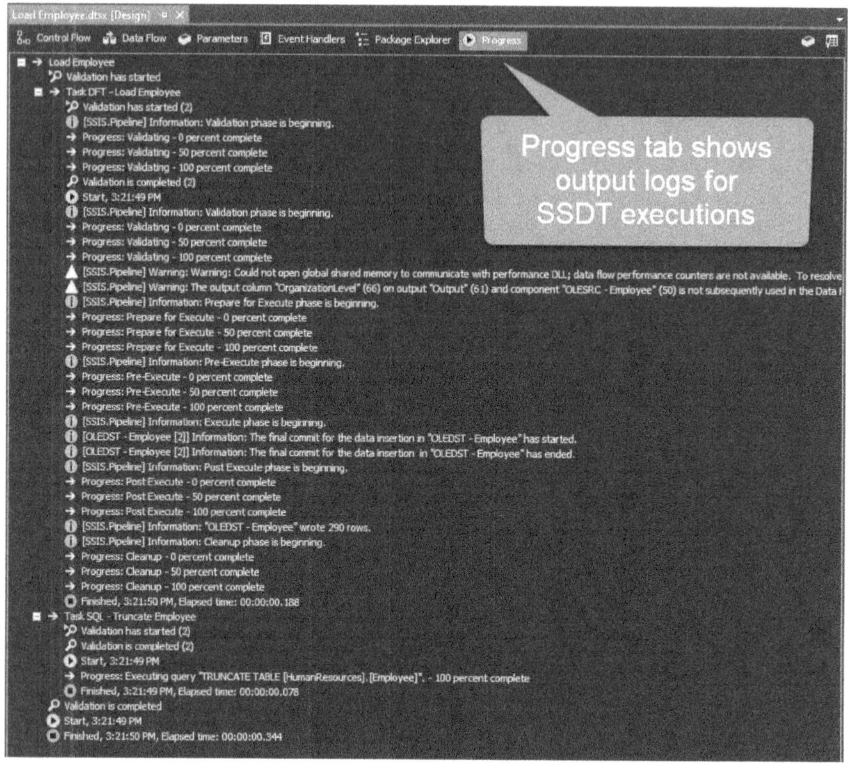

Package Validation

Built into the SQL Server Integration Services catalog is the ability to run a validation without actually executing the package. Running a package validation in the SSIS catalog performs a high-level check against the underlying metadata to check for common points of failure (especially those related to data flows). This validation process is not designed to capture every metadata issue, but it can help identify some issues to avoid runtime surprises.

Validation can be run manually from SSMS, like how one would run the package. Right-clicking the package name reveals, among other items, the Validate menu selection.

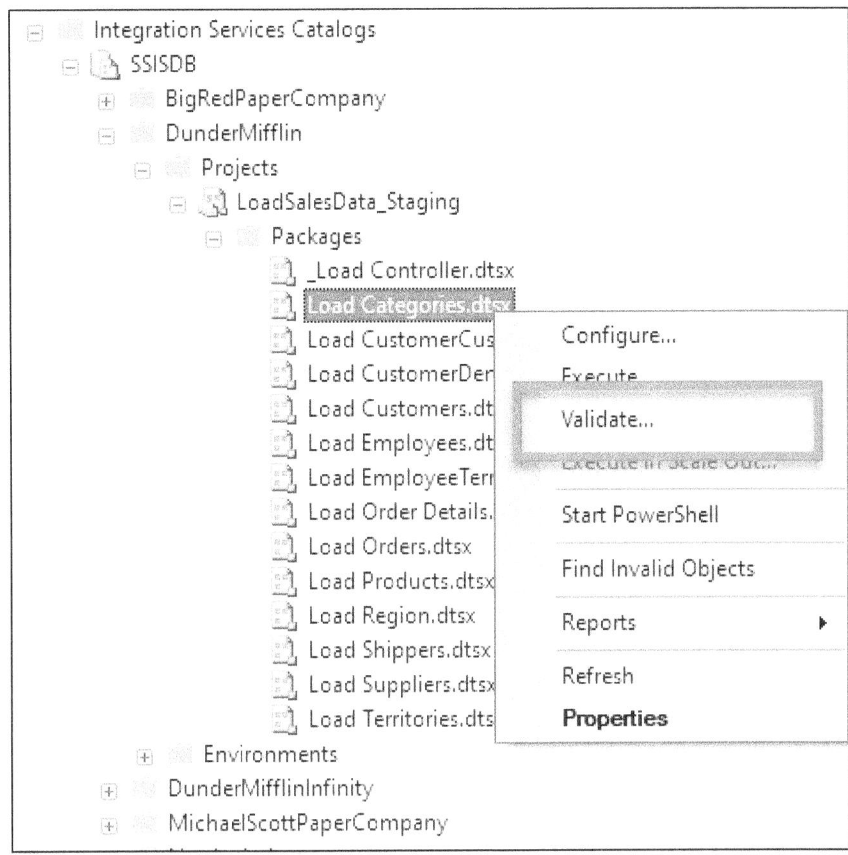

The Validate Package window, shown below, looks like a trimmed-down version of the Execute Package window.

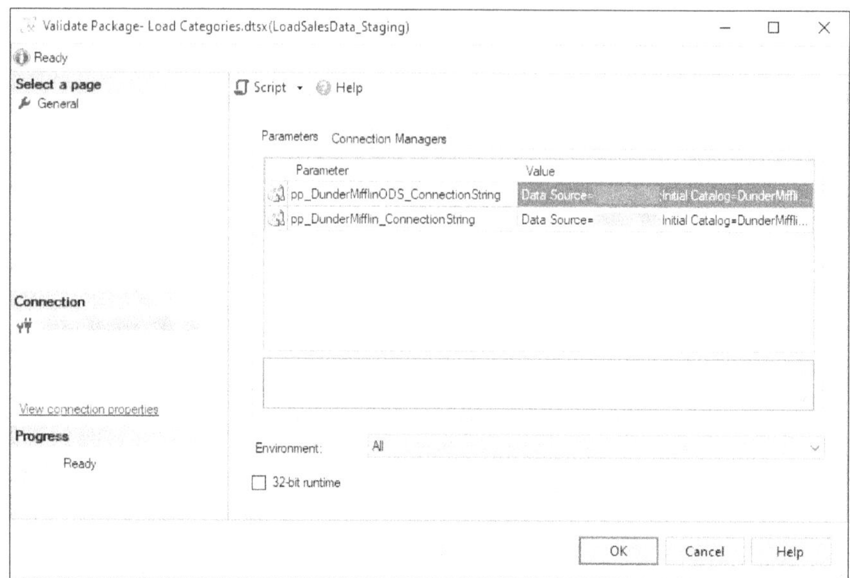

When you start this validation, you can go to the output report which will show the results of the validation along with any errors found.

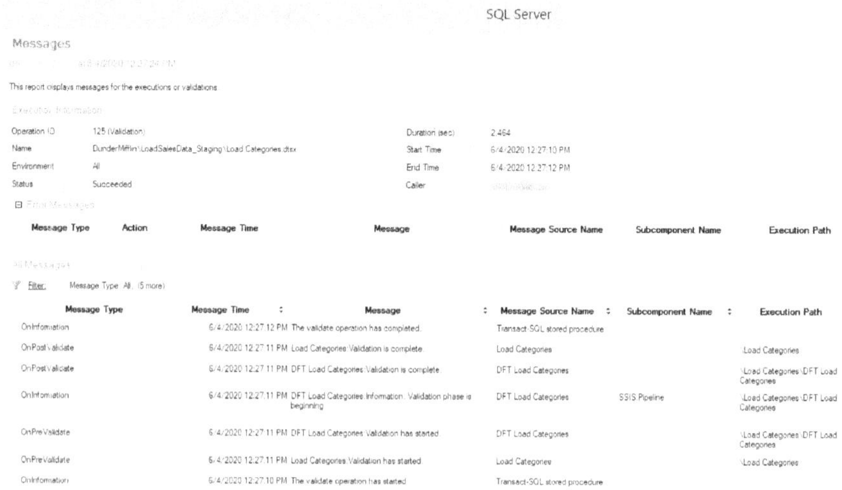

Like most other SSIS catalog operations, this one can be run through T-SQL as well. As shown below, the `[validate_package]` stored procedure will invoke the package validation.

```sql
USE SSISDB;

DECLARE @validation_id BIGINT;

EXEC [catalog].[validate_package]
      @package_name = N'Load Categories.dtsx'
      , @validation_id = @validation_id OUTPUT
      , @folder_name = N'DunderMifflin'
      , @project_name = N'LoadSalesData_Staging'
      , @use32bitruntime = False
      , @environment_scope = A
      , @reference_id = NULL;

GO
```

The results of the validation can be retrieved using the view
`[catalog].[validations]`. Status is reported in the `status_id`
column using the same values used by package executions: 7 represents
success, 4 indicates failure, etc. It is worth noting that there is also a
stored procedure to perform a similar validation on an entire project
(`[catalog].[validate_project]`).

When the SSIS package validation is performed, it will check *some* of the
package metadata. I want to reiterate that it doesn't check everything,
nor does a successful validation guarantee a successful package
execution. The scope of validation is concentrated mostly on data flow
components, looking for unexpected changes in column metadata,
missing tables, or invalid connections. A package validation will also
check that a needed connection is present, though it will usually not
indicate an error if that connection is offline. A package validation
normally does not fail when a source file is missing or a directory path is
invalid, either.

So for all of the things that a package validation doesn't do, what value
does it offer? Here's an ideal use case: If you work in an environment
where database metadata is prone to change, and you're weary of
being awakened with VS_NEEDSNEWMETADATA errors in the middle of
the night, running package validations can help to identify those issues
before the package is actually executed. Running a validation against a
package is also very useful in automated testing scenarios, in which you

perform a validation and then check the status of that validation before going more deeply into the process.

Chapter 5

Configurations, Parameters, and Environments

One of the most notable changes brought about by the introduction of the SSIS catalog was the introduction of parameters and environments.

In older versions of SSIS, package configurations were used to supply runtime values for attributes of a package that could change over time (such as connection strings, file paths, and login credentials) to SSIS packages. Using these external credentials would reduce the number of code changes required when these attributes would change by decoupling the source code from the runtime values that would naturally change over time. While it was easy to set up an individual configuration for a package, from an enterprise management perspective, these configurations were opaque and decentralized, with little if any administrative control or visibility into when and how configurations were used. Further, it was frighteningly easy to store sensitive configuration information such as passwords in plain text.

Unfortunately, there was no easy way to ensure that a particular configuration value be supplied at runtime, and if the package was executed without it, it could fail with an obscure error, or even worse, would succeed with the incorrect default value. This was even more challenging if you wanted to invoke a child package from a parent package, since the child package would not expose the list of runtime values it would expect to receive from a parent package.

SSIS Parameters

Starting with the release of SQL Server 2012, Integration Services came equipped with parameters to allow the package developer to configure placeholders for values to be supplied at runtime. These parameters could be set at the package level (visible only to that package) or at the project level (accessible by any package in the project), and could be marked as either optional or required. Parameters added much-needed modularity to SSIS package execution.

Since we're focusing just on the SSIS catalog in this book, I won't spend a lot of time on parameter usage in package design. However, I will illustrate briefly how parameters are used in package execution, and more specific to the SSIS catalog, how parameters are grouped together into SSIS catalog environments.

What are SSIS Catalog Environments?

Simply put, an SSIS catalog environment (or more commonly, just *environment*) is a collection of related variables. Each environment can be referenced by one or more projects, and in turn, the variables in those environments can be mapped to the project or package parameters in each project.

Using environments to assign runtime values to parameters can take some of the manual work out of package execution. If you had a package with 15 parameters, for example, you would need to provide values for each one of those parameters each time the package was run. However, if you were to create and environment with 15 variables (one for each of the parameters for that package), you'd only need to specify the environment ID when executing the package each time. Environments are also reusable across projects, which can reduce the number of environments you'd need to create.

Are SSIS catalog environments the same as the environment variables from legacy SSIS configurations?

No, they are two different things entirely, although they serve a similar purpose. Before SQL Server 2012, one had to use SSIS configurations to pass in dynamic runtime values, and one of the options available for this was to use a Windows machine environment variable to store the value to provide to the package at runtime. SSIS catalog environments also work to supply runtime values, but the way in which they work is completely different from the legacy environment variables.

This is one of those cases in which Microsoft could have (and frankly, should have) eliminated some of the ambiguity by naming SSIS catalog environments differently. The good news is that the legacy environment variable settings are no longer visible by default in packages configured for deployment to the SSIS catalog. When you see references to an environment in this book, assume that it refers to the SSIS catalog environment and not to the legacy configuration bearing a similar name.

Creating an SSIS Catalog Environment

To build and configure an SSIS catalog environment requires four relatively simple steps: create the environment; add the variables to the environment; add a reference to the environment for the project; and finally, specify which environment variables match up to each of the parameters. Each of the above steps can be done either in the UI in SSMS, or through T-SQL script using built-in stored procedures in the SSIS catalog.

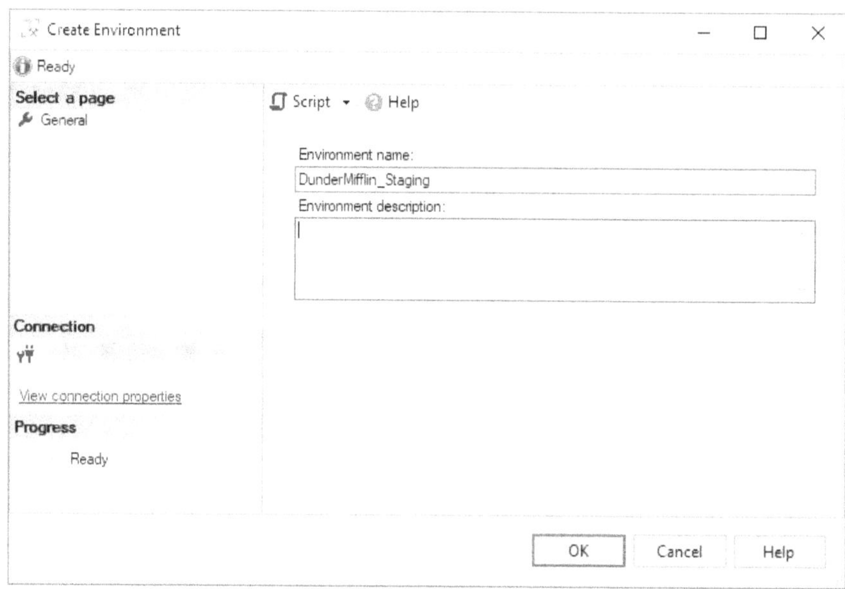

Shown above is the dialog box for creating an SSIS catalog environment. Note that you can create an environment in any of the user-created folder, and the new environment will show up in the Environments virtual subfolder (more on those virtual folders in the next section).

Once the environment is created, you can add one or more variables.

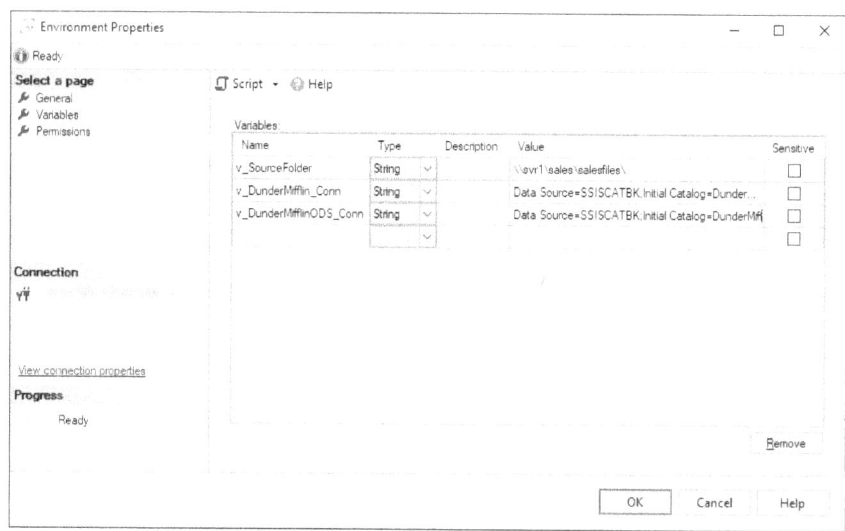

Once all the variables have been added, that completes the setup of the environment.

> ### *What is the Sensitive check box on the environment variable?*
>
> Most of the variable values you'll store in your SSIS environment variables can be safely stored as plain text. However, there are some values that need to be specifically protected, including passwords, API keys, and other secrets. Those values should never be stored in plain text and must be encrypted at rest.
>
> When you enable the Sensitive setting on an SSIS environment variable, that value will be stored not as plain text but as an encrypted value. Under the hood, the SSIS runtime can decrypt and use the sensitive value when the package is run, but an ordinary user can't read this value in the underlying table.
>
> When you turn on the Sensitive property for an SSIS environment variable, make sure you also have the password stored securely in your password management system. Because the value is encrypted before it is stored in the SSISDB database, it cannot be decrypted by a user without the database encryption key.
>
> One final note about sensitive variables: you can only map a variable marked as Sensitive to a parameter that was also set as Sensitive in the package or project. Because runtime parameter values are logged to the SSISDB database (more on that in the next chapter on logging), allowing a sensitive value to be used as plain text in the package would prevent a security risk. Be aware that the variable-to-parameter mapping window will let you set it up that way, but you'll get an error when the package is run for any sensitive variables mapped to unsecured parameters.

Before you can use this new SSIS catalog environment as part of a package execution, you'll need to configure the project to add a reference to that new environment. You'll find the Configure window by right-clicking the project and selecting Configure.

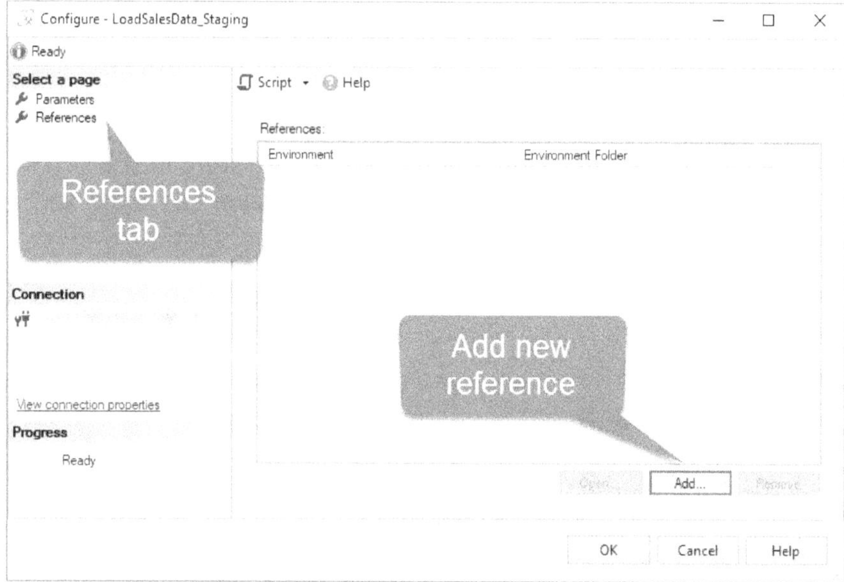

Click Add to create a new reference from the selected project and browse to find the environment you just created. You can reference any environment in the SSIS catalog, not just the one in the same folder as the project.

Once you have created a project reference to that environment, you can edit the parameter mappings. Shown below is the default setting, where the parameters are set to static values.

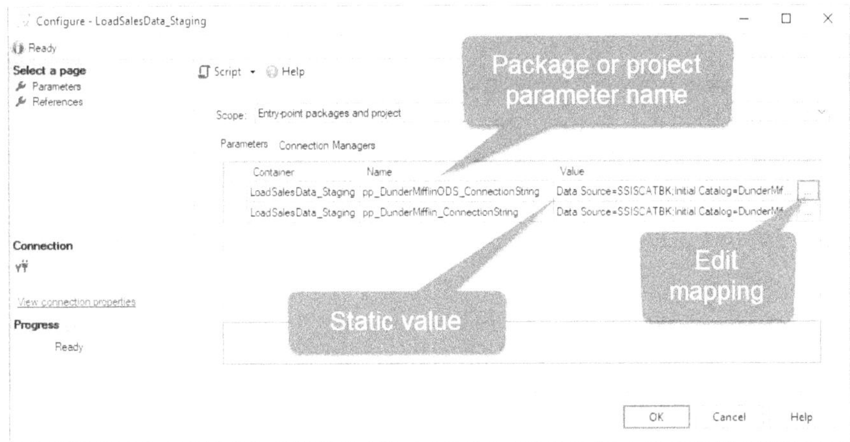

Finally, you can click the ellipsis on the right to map an environment variable to the parameter value. Repeat this process for each parameter that will get its runtime value from a variable in this environment.

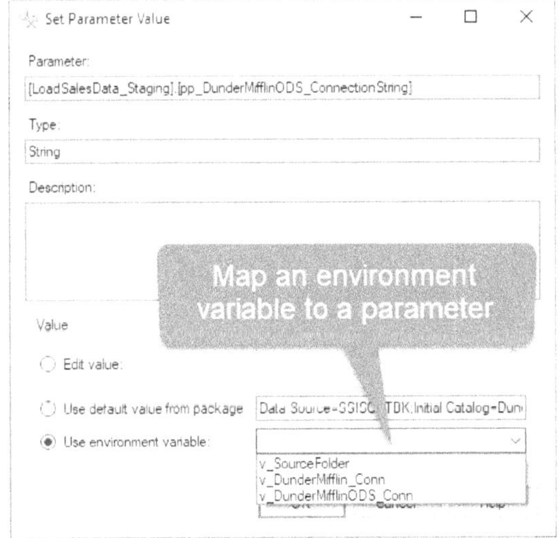

Once the reference has been created and the variables mapped to parameters, you'll then be able to use the environment when executing a package in that project. I'll demonstrate how to reference an environment during package execution in the next chapter.

Even after you map an environment variable to a parameter, you'll still be able to specify a static value for that parameter if needed.

Using an Environment in a Package Execution

Once you have created and configured the environment for use on your SSIS project(s), it can then be used any time you execute one of the packages in that project. Adding an environment to a package execution is very easy, and can be done interactively through the user interface, via T-SQL, or in a SQL Server Agent job step.

SSMS UI Execution with Environment Reference

Shown below is the UI for executing a package manually from SSMS. This is similar to the example shown in the previous chapter, but has a couple of warnings for missing parameter values. Since I have set up a reference to an environment and variable mappings for each of the parameters, this package expects to have a runtime value specified.

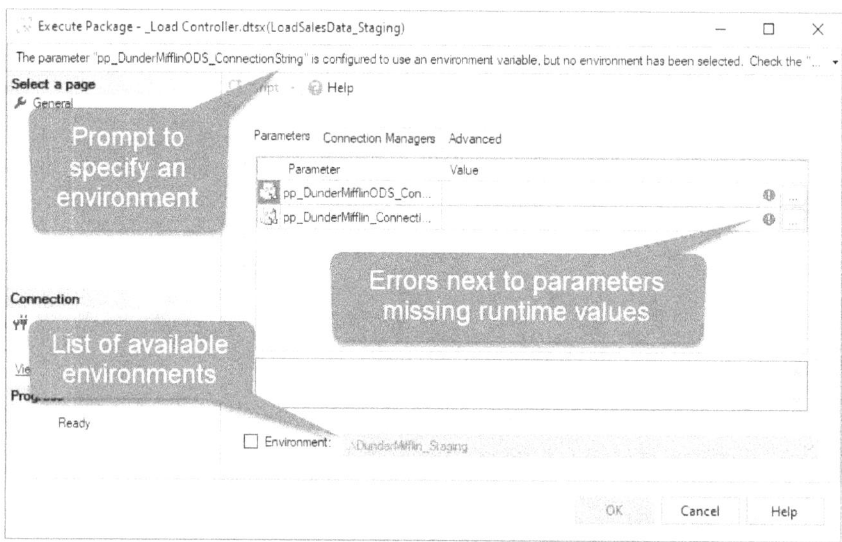

Here you can check the box next to the Environment selection at the bottom and select one of the mapped environments (in this case, there is just one available) to apply the variables in that environment to the parameters for a single execution. Checking that box will clear all the errors on this dialog box as shown below, allowing you to execute the package.

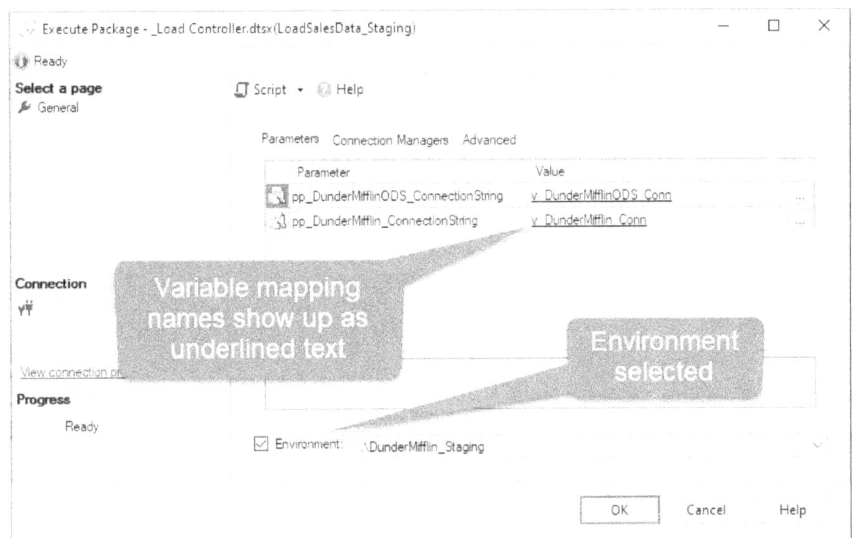

In the Parameters window above, the type of text decoration in the Value field indicates the source of the runtime value. If the text is underlined as shown, this indicates the value is derived from an environment variable. Bold text indicates a statically defined value. Plain text (neither bolded nor underlined) indicates the use of design-time default values.

T-SQL Execution with Environment Reference

Using T-SQL to execute a package that includes an SSIS catalog environment for configuration is a simple process. To do so adds one additional step to the typical T-SQL execution workflow: you must first get the environment reference ID. The following code queries the `[catalog].[environment_references]` table to get that ID value.

```sql
USE SSISDB
GO

DECLARE @projNm NVARCHAR(100)
      , @envNm NVARCHAR(100)

SET @projNm = N'LoadSalesData_Staging'
SET @envNm = N'DunderMifflin_Staging'

SELECT r.reference_id
FROM catalog.environment_references r
```

```sql
INNER JOIN catalog.projects p
       ON p.project_id = r.project_id
WHERE p.name = @projNm
AND r.environment_name = @envNm
```

The reference_id value is needed for the execution step. Using the stored procedure [catalog].[create_execution] shown in the previous chapter, I'll pass in the reference_id from the above script. This is the functional equivalent of setting the Environment from the available list in the SSMS UI.

```sql
-- Create the execution
DECLARE @x_id BIGINT;

EXEC [catalog].[create_execution]
       @package_name = N'_Load Controller.dtsx'
     , @execution_id = @x_id OUTPUT
     , @folder_name = N'DunderMifflin'
     , @project_name = N'LoadSalesData_Staging'
     , @use32bitruntime = False
     , @reference_id = @envNm     -- Environment ref ID here
     , @runinscaleout = False

-- Start the package execution
EXEC [catalog].[start_execution] @execution_id = @x_id
```

Setting the reference_id parameter for the [create_execution] stored procedure will cause the specified environment to be used for this execution.

Execution via SQL Server Agent using Environment Reference

Using an environment reference in a SQL Server Agent job step is almost identical to the process for doing so with a manual execution through SSMS. Simply tick the Environment checkbox and select the environment to use.

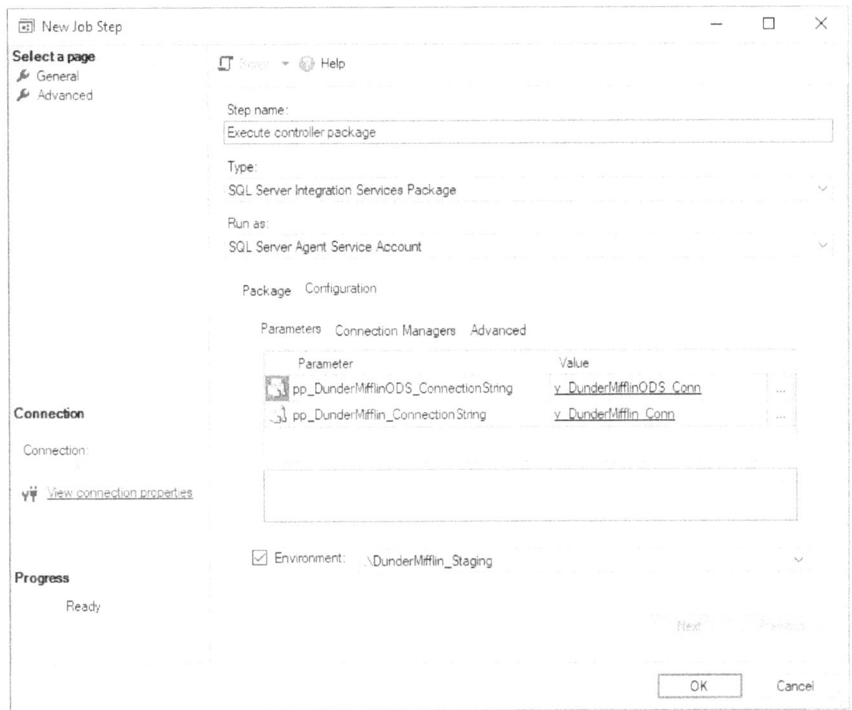

When you set up the SQL Server Agent job step to use the environment for this package, the same environment will be used each time this job step is executed.

Final Thoughts on SSIS Catalog Environments

Here are a few things to keep in mind when creating and using SSIS catalog environments:

- An environment is not exclusive to any particular SSIS project, nor vice versa. A single project can be configured to use one of any number of environments, and each environment can be referenced by an unlimited number of projects.

- For any single execution, you can only use one environment. This is one of the few shortcomings of the SSIS catalog environments. I wish it were possible to apply more than one environment for a single execution to allow for more targeted groupings of variables, similar to what we could do with legacy package configurations in older versions of SSIS.

- Configuring a project with an environment reference does not mean that this environment will automatically be used when a package in that project is executed. Even after creating the reference and setting the variable-to-parameter mappings, you still have to direct the execution to use that environment via the UI or script.

- When using an environment to supply parameter values, you can still set individual parameters manually. If you use an environment that sets a parameter and then you explicitly specify a parameter value, the latter will take precedence over the former for that parameter value.

- When you redeploy an existing project to the SSIS catalog, all the existing environment references and variable-to-parameter mappings will be preserved.

Chapter 6

Execution Logging

Logging, admittedly, is one of the duller topics in the technical world, and it's no more exciting in SSIS than it is anywhere else. However, having a good logging mechanism is essential to making SSIS processes easier to develop, troubleshoot, and monitor.

With older versions (pre-2012), logging was much more challenging, because it had to be set up on a package-by-package basis. With the SSIS catalog, though, logging is much easier to automate, and almost becomes a "set it and forget it" operation.

SSIS Catalog Logging Basics

When the SSIS catalog was introduced with the release of SQL Server 2012, it fundamentally changed the way SSIS package executions are logged. Gone was the need go through tedious pages of UI checkboxes to capture ETL status, runtimes, and informational messages; the logging of these events happens automatically by default.

The particulars of logging could now be changed as a runtime setting without modifying or even opening the package. By using one of four predefined logging levels, defining the depth of how much information to log became as simple as choosing a selection from a drop-down list. Using built-in SSIS catalog logging required surrendering granular control over which logging events you wanted to capture, but it was a small price to pay for the ease of catalog logging.

Built-In Reports

One of the easily recognizable advantages of SSIS catalog logging is the inclusion of built-in reports that present package execution information in an easy-to-digest format. Using these reports, one can see a snapshot of what's happening right now, get an overview of prior executions, or drill into a specific SSIS load for troubleshooting purposes.

The built-in SSIS catalog reports are accessible from within the Integration Services Catalogs node within SSMS. If you right-click on this SSISDB folder within that node and drill through the Reports subfolder, you'll see the report options available to you.

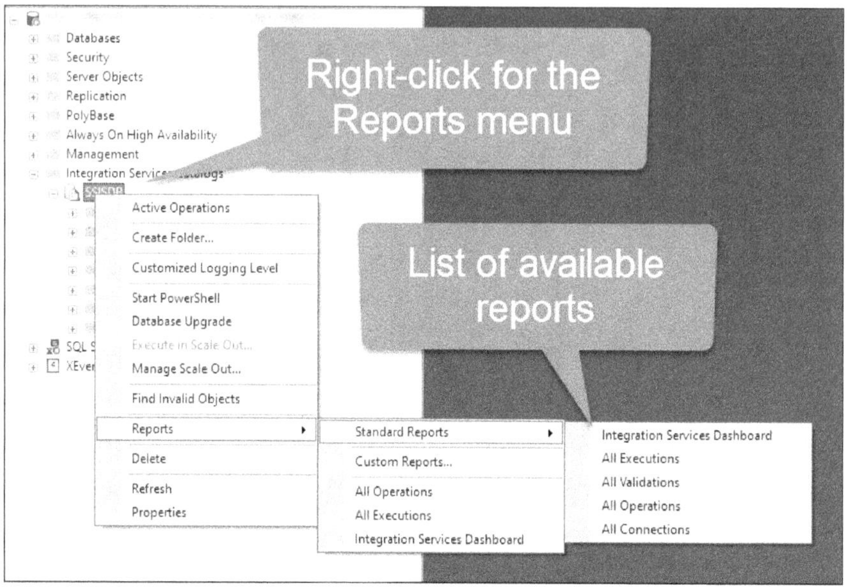

The first of these options is the Integration Services Dashboard, which is a great first stop for looking at current activity and recent history. This view shows what is currently running as well as a count and a list of packages that have run in the past 24 hours.

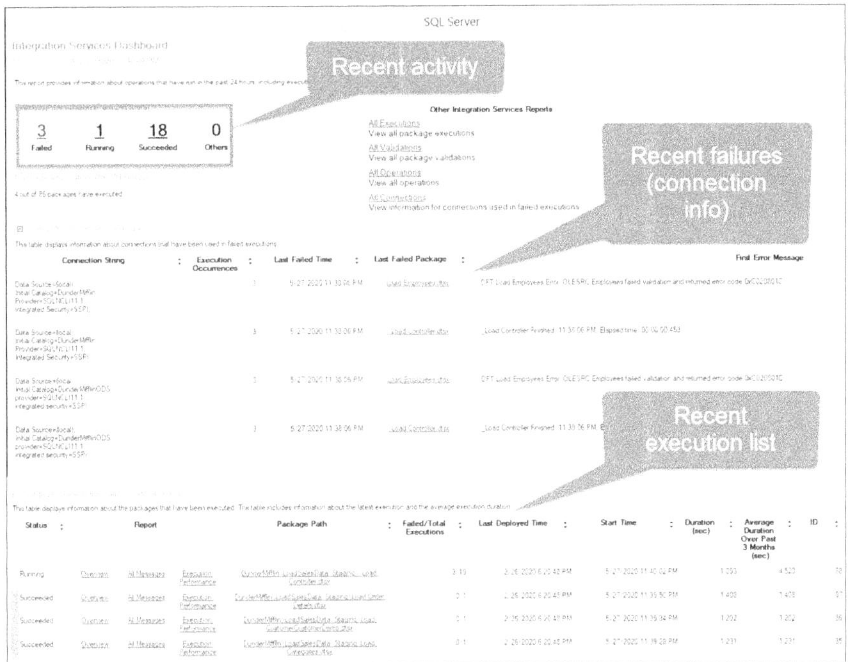

As shown, this instance of SSIS has run 18 successful packages, three package failures, and one currently running. You'll notice there is more information that will fit on a single screen; scrolling down or to the right will reveal more detail, including a list of the successful package executions at the bottom of this report.

Each of the other report menu items will take you to a report on executions, validations, operations (which includes deployments), and connections, respectively. The most common of these is the All Executions, which displays all the recent executions.

This view provides a useful glimpse into the most recent executions: by default, the history from the past 7 days is shown. Unlike the dashboard report, though, this one allows you to change the date range on the filter to show more than just that limited time frame.

When running these reports through the SSISDB node, you'll see all the activity for the entire SSIS catalog. However, if you are interested in only a subset – a folder, a project, or even a single package – you can drill down to the specific asset you want to see to limit the scope of your search. Right-clicking an item deeper in the folder structure as shown below shows the reporting data filtered to that item and anything below it.

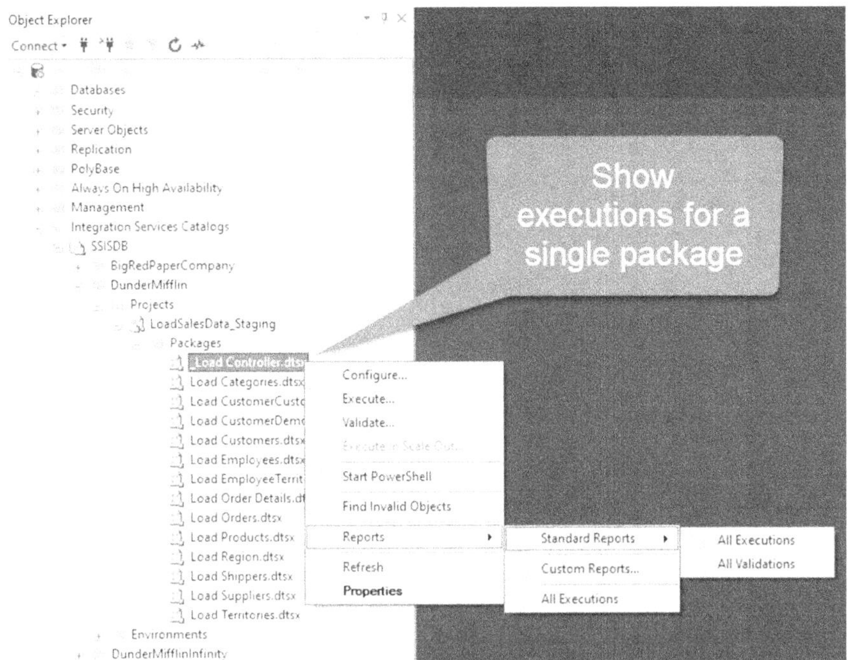

Most of these reports contain links to allow deeper exploration into failures and other anomalies. For example, the All Executions report allows you to click through to the Execution Overview report, showing the details (including any error or warning messages) of a single execution.

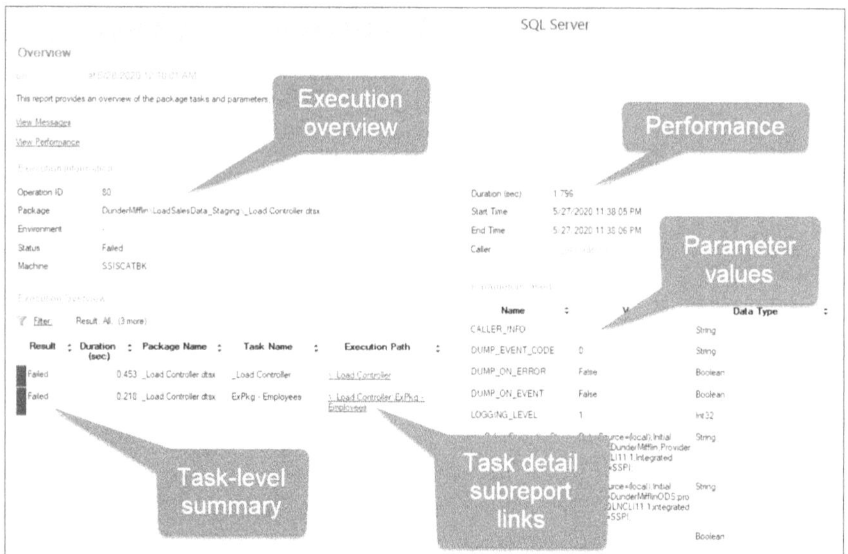

These built-in reports are useful for quick analysis of recent activity. However, in using the built-in SSIS catalog reports, there are a few shortcomings:

- The user running the reports must have a specific set of permissions beyond simple read-only access to the SSISDB database

- The built-in reports are hard-coded and cannot be modified

- The reports are only available from within SQL Server Management Studio

- The data in these reports cannot be exported. You can print the report (to a page or a PDF document), but that is the extent of the export capability.

- You can't even select the text to copy elsewhere (such as a search engine to look for errors or other anomaly information).

The good news is that all the data shown in the packaged catalog reports is simply stored in logging tables in the SSIS catalog database (SSISDB). With a basic understanding of the underlying logging tables, one can write queries or build their own customized reports for displaying status and history information.

SSIS Catalog Logging Views

There are several dozen views in the SSISDB database, but you only need to understand a handful of them to be proficient at package execution analysis. Below I list and explain some of these essential logging views.

> ### Aren't there also tables with this same information?
>
> Yes, for each of the views mentioned below, there is a table with the same name, except that each of those tables resides in the `[internal]` schema. For users who have permission to query the SSIS database, it's actually a bit easier to query these views than the underlying tables, since the views abstract the table data in a very reporting-friendly way. My recommendation is to use the views unless you encounter a need that requires to go directly to the table to retrieve.

`[catalog].[operations]`

The operations view displays each high-level operation that occurs in the SSIS catalog. Here you'll find meta information such as the operation ID, when the operation began and when it completed (if it did), the status of the operation, and who performed the operation. Note that this doesn't just store SSIS package executions; also available in this view is a log of project deployments, project restores, changes to global properties of the catalog, and package validations, among other operations.

Operations logs are available in this view regardless of which logging level you choose (even if you pick the logging level "None").

The status values are displayed by numerical ID, but oddly, there is no lookup table in the SSISDB database to show which IDs translate to which status values. The script at **TimMitchell.net/go/ssis-exec-status-list** is one I wrote to manually create an execution status lookup table for ease of reporting.

`[catalog].[executions]`

This view lists each of the package executions that has been created in the SSIS catalog. Information in this view includes the execution ID, the path to the package, the catalog environment (if one was used for this execution), and whether the 32-bit runtime was used for the execution.

It is important to note that there are a couple of execution types that will not show up in the executions view:

- *Packages executed using the Execute Package Task in SSIS.* Packages executed using this task are still logged, but each of their tasks and components is logged as part of the parent package and does not show a distinct execution record in `[catalog].[executions]`. When you look for details on a child package invoked in this way, you'll need to look for executions of the parent package, where you will find the execution details for the child package log entries as a subset of the logs for the Execute Package Task that invoked it.

- *Packages executed in SQL Server Data Tools (SSDT).* As noted earlier, because a package execution within SSDT is not truly a catalog execution, it is not logged in the catalog logging tables. Only package executions invoked from the SSIS catalog are logged in these tables.

This view will be used in most every query you write against the SSISDB database. The execution object is the centerpiece of such reporting, so this view will be a key part of the solution. Get it know it well.

`[catalog].[executable_statistics]`

This view lists the execution summary for each executable; that is, every task or container in an executed SSIS package. Here you'll find the full path to the executable object within the package, start and completion times, duration, and the execution result (stored as a simple

1 or 0 for failure or success, respectively). This view is useful for identifying task-level failures or bottlenecks.

`[catalog].[execution_component_phases]`

This view is useful for showing runtime statistics about individual data flow components. The execution_component_phases view shows each execution phase of every data flow component, showing very granular information about each step (or phase) of the component execution. This can be a very busy table, especially if you've got a lot of data flow components or you have a data flow running many times within a loop.

Runtime data is logged here only in Performance or Verbose logging modes.

`[catalog].[execution_data_statistics]`

This view shows row counts of data moved through an SSIS data flow. Each "leg" of the pipeline will be represented here, with each row in the log table indicating the source component, destination component, when the log entry was created, and how many rows were processed. Keep in mind that each row in this view shows a single buffer of data, so for a large load you'll have multiple log entries per leg of the pipeline.

This log table is only written to when using Verbose logging mode.

`[catalog].[operation_messages]`
and `[catalog].[event_messages]`

I've grouped these views together because they are typically used together. The operation_messages table contains the text of detailed messages in the log, while event_message stores some of the metadata belonging to that message. The operation_messages view captures information about package executions, validations, and a few other operations (such as restoring an older version of a project), while event_message is specific to package executions and logs information about the package itself.

These views are used for package executions set to any logging level except None.

`[catalog].[execution_message_context]`

The event_message_context view shows many of the implicit runtime settings for packages and connections. Many of the settings from the package properties are included here, as well as the details from each package and project connection. This view has some usefulness when performing deep debugging, or for checking for packages that are not in compliance with company guidelines (such as using a specific Package Protection Level in the source code).

On very busy SSIS servers, the information shown in this view can become quite voluminous. Make sure you keep an eye on the amount of information that collects in the underlying table, as it can grow very large when you run a lot of frequent package executions on the SSIS catalog.

`[catalog].[execution_parameter_values]`

The execution_parameter_values view lists the parameters passed to a package execution. Both package and project level parameters are shown here, as well as system parameters that may be implicitly or explicitly specified. This log view is useful for tracking down why a package failed by analyzing the runtime values it was passed (another great reason to parameterize your packages).

One of the security features of SSIS is that it masks sensitive pieces of information. That includes this view, which has an encrypted column (defined in the underlying table) for storing passwords or any other runtime parameter explicitly marked as Sensitive. Parameter values that are marked as Sensitive will be logged as encrypted values, and those without such designation (which is the default behavior) are logged in plain text. As such, make sure you always mark as Sensitive any parameters that contain information that should be protected in logging.

Runtime parameter values will be shown in this view for any package execution in the catalog, regardless of the logging level specified.

`[catalog].[validations]`

The validations view shows the results of validation operations that are performed on packages or projects. If you have as part of your execution or workflow a process to run validations against your SSIS packages, you should include this data set in your logging reports.

The amount of information written to the SSIS catalog logging tables depends on the logging level selected. Unlike the logging structures in older versions of SSIS, the logging level is specified for every execution, allowing you to easily change to a different logging level with no code changes.

There are five built-in logging levels in the SSIS catalog:

- **None**. This logging level doesn't really turn off logging as the name implies. With this logging level, only the package execution itself is logged (including start time, end time, and status), and none of the details are captured. This logging level has the least amount of overhead, but does not give you much information to use for troubleshooting or debugging.

- **Basic**. This is the default logging level, and will write both package and task execution information to the log. This level also captures warning and informational messages. For most operations, the Basic logging level is sufficient.

- **Performance**. Like the basic logging, the performance logging level will also capture task-level information. However, this setting limits the types of messages captured (including only warnings and errors), and also provides more detailed information about data flow components not included in Basic logging. The performance logging level can be useful during testing (especially performance testing, as implied by its name), but I've not had the need to use this setting for a normal, scheduled package execution.

- **Verbose**. If you want to capture everything going on with your package execution, verbose logging level is the way to go. Using this setting for your package execution will capture all messages and events that occur during the execution, and has the added advantage of logging data flow row counts as well. However, I'd caution you to use this under a watchful eye: verbose logging level generates a lot of output in the logging tables, sometimes thousands or even tens of thousands of new log rows for a single execution! Verbose logging mode is best suited for manual package executions when you are trying to get to the root of a specific problem within the package.

- **RuntimeLineage**. This logging level was first introduced with SQL Server 2016, and captures some artifacts of data lineage within data flows. However, the information written using this logging level is a poor substitute for proper data lineage documentation, and does not paint a complete picture of what most organizations require in terms of data lineage. Other than for demonstration purposes, I have not found any real use for this logging level.

Custom Logging Levels

Although the built-in logging levels allowed a much simpler logging experience than the old manual style of logging in package deployment mode, there isn't any flexibility in what each of those logging levels will capture. Fortunately, this changed starting with SQL Server 2016 with the introduction of custom logging levels.

Custom logging levels allow you to set up your own customized list of metrics and events as a reusable framework for capturing only those logging data points you need.

Custom logging levels are not specific to any package or project. Each of these custom logging levels is set up on the SSIS catalog itself, and may be used when executing any package in that catalog.

Setting up a custom logging level is a very simple process. Right-click on the SSISDB node in the Integration Services Catalogs folder in SSMS and choose Customized Logging Level. The Customized Logging Level Management window allows you to create a new or edit an existing logging level. Highlighting the desired level in the Customized Logging Level list will let you edit the statistics and events that will be logged when using that custom logging level. You can create a new logging level here as well, and even start with the settings for a built-in logging level as a template.

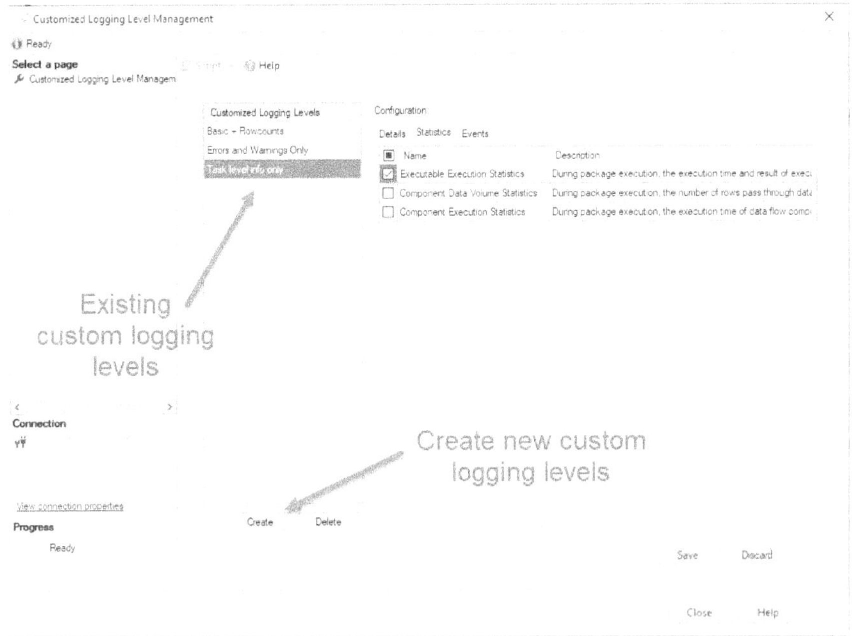

If you want a step-by-step walkthrough on setting up a new custom logging level, you can visit my blog post on that topic at **TimMitchell.net/go/customlogginglevels**.

When executing a package from the SSIS catalog, you'll have the option of specifying the logging level (either a built-in logging level or a custom logging level). As shown below in the Execute Package dialog box, the option to select the logging level is set for a single execution. Note that you'll have a similar set of options when you set up a SQL Server Agent job step to execute a package. When setting up that job step, the log setting you specify will be used for each execution of that package from that job step.

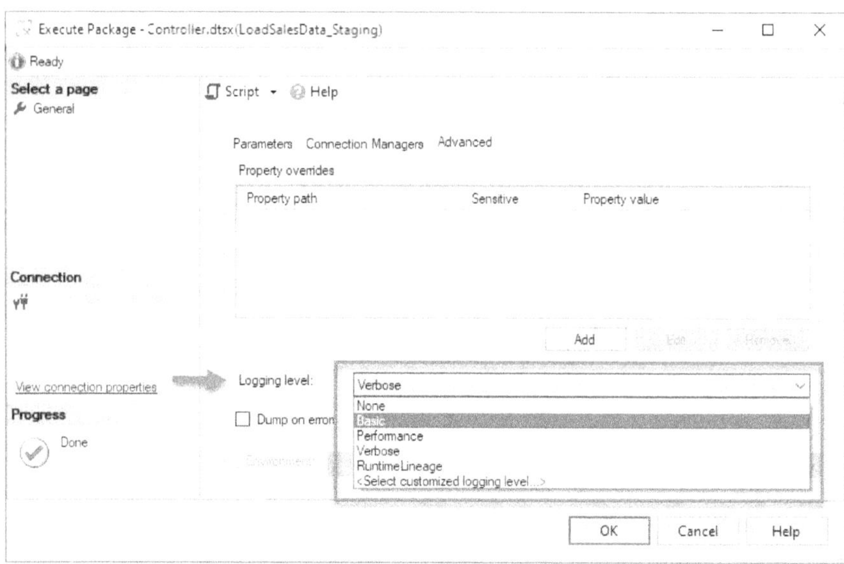

The selection will look a little different if you select a custom logging level. If you pick that selection, you'll be presented with a list of custom logging levels that have been created on the SSIS catalog, and you can pick the one you want to use from that list.

Server-Wide Default Logging Level

If you do not choose a logging level for a package execution or job step, it will default to the server-wide default logging level set in the SSIS catalog properties. As shown below, this is initially set to Basic, but you can change this to default to any logging level you choose (even a custom logging level).

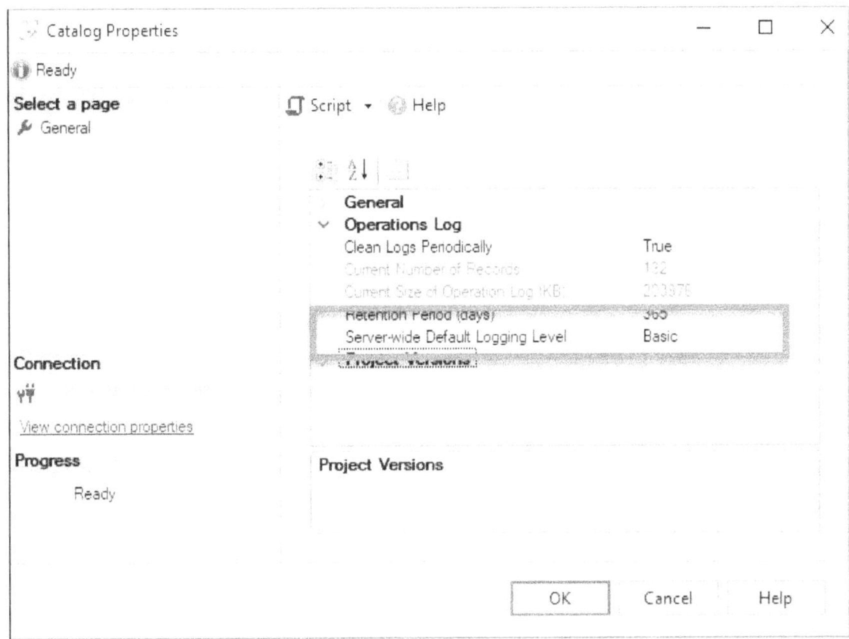

This setting is simply the default to be used absent any other selection. You'll still be able to pick any of the built-in or custom logging levels when creating a new execution.

Data Taps

The data tap is a very handy mechanism within an SSIS package execution. A data tap works similarly to the way a data viewer would work when executing a package from SSDT, but instead of simply displaying the data on the screen, the data is stored in a file.

With a data tap, you can specify that a particular execution will write out the data passing through one of the "legs" of the data flow out to a CSV file. This is incredibly useful when debugging a deployed package, as it allows you a glimpse into the in-flight data within a data flow without requiring you to open the package at all.

Here's how a data tap works:

- You create (but do not yet start) an execution in the SSIS catalog, using the `[catalog].[create_execution]` stored procedure.

- You'll then set up the data tap for that execution by calling the `[catalog].[add_data_tap]` stored procedure, passing in as parameters the execution ID, the execution path to the data flow to be tapped, and the name of the dataflow path (the "leg" of the data flow) to be written to the data tap. You'll also specify the output filename and, if you wish to limit the size of the output file, the maximum number of rows to be written to that file.

- Start the package execution by invoking the stored procedure `[catalog].[start_execution]`. The data for the specified data flow and path will be written to the file.

If the data flow executes successfully, you'll find the data from the specified data flow path written to a CSV with the file name you provided.

Adding a data tap only modifies that one execution, not the package itself. Therefore, if you execute the same package again without adding a data tap, it will execute normally. You have to explicitly set up a data tap for each execution.

There are a few things to be aware of when using data taps:

- There is no user interface for managing data taps. To set up an execution and add a data tap, you must use T-SQL to invoke SSIS catalog stored procedures.

- The data tap is hard-coded to write to a specified SQL Server folder. Although you will specify the file name when setting up the data tap, the output file will always be written to the folder **\Program Files\Microsoft SQL Server\<ver>\DTS\DataDumps** where <ver> is the version of SQL Server you are using (for example, 140 for SQL Server 2017).

- You'll have to know a little about the SSIS package structure to set up the data tap. Because you must pass in parameters for the execution path to the data flow and the identification string for the specific data flow path to tap, you'll have to either query the SSIS catalog for prior execution logs or open up the SSIS package in SSDT to get the data flow path identifiers.

- When you use a data tap, you need to be especially aware of the sensitivity of the data you are handling. Make sure the output folder is properly secured, and that you are not inadvertently storing data that would violate laws (HIPAA, PCI, etc.) or company policy.

For a step-by-step example of how to set up a data tap, visit **TimMitchell.net/go/datataps**.

Chapter 7

Enterprise Management and Administration of the SSIS Catalog

Getting started with the SSIS catalog is relatively easy. Creating the catalog, setting up a few folders, and deploying and executing a project can be done in minutes. However, the SSIS catalog is an enterprise ETL component, and must be integrated as such.

In this chapter, I'll cover some of the enterprise management and administration concerns, including log retention, backup and restore of the SSISDB database, and scaling out SSIS executions.

SSISDB Log Retention

By far, the bulk of the SSISDB database is in the logging tables. Over time, package executions and other logged operations fill the logging tables with detailed information about SSIS catalog activity. While this log information is valuable, It loses its value over time, with the oldest log data having far less value than the more recent data.

To prevent a situation in which overgrown log tables start to impact other parts of the architecture, the SSIS catalog is equipped with a retention mechanism that will delete old data from the log tables. The purge process is set by default to run each day, deleting log entries for events older than 365 days.

The log retention settings are configured in the SSISDB catalog properties. As highlighted below, these properties are found in the Catalog Properties window for the SSIS catalog.

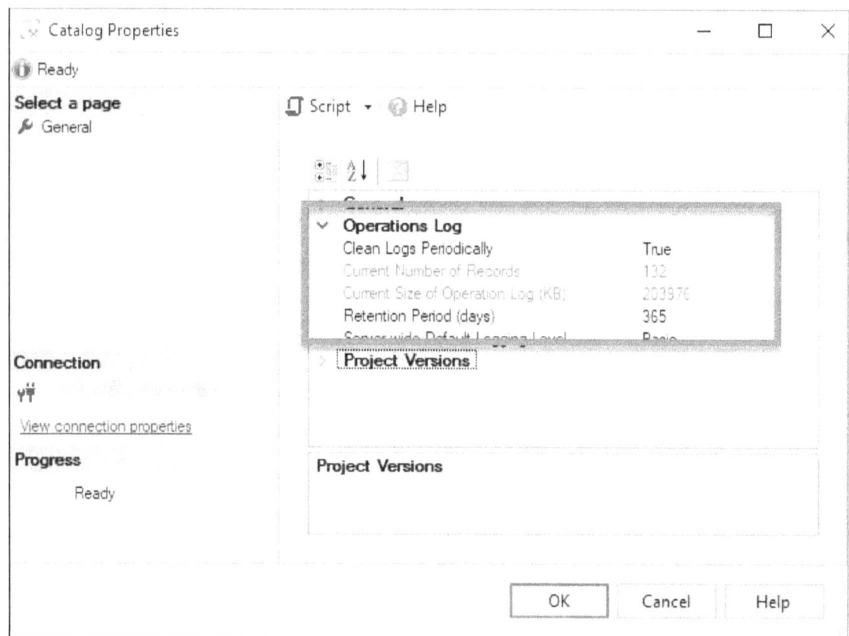

When the Clean Logs Periodically setting is set to True, the process to clean up the log entries outside the retention window will be run each day at midnight. This is done through a SQL Server Agent job named *SSIS Server Maintenance Job* that is created automatically when the SSIS catalog is created.

Performance Issues with Log Purge

For most SSIS catalog databases with a modest level of activity, the daily operation to run this log purge will run without any issues. However, if you've got a large amount of data – either from using an aggressive logging level or a large number of executions – you may encounter performance issues when this log purge process runs.

One reason for this is the default scheduled time for the purge job. It is scheduled to run at midnight, which is a very common time to schedule overnight operations. This could lead to contention issues, with the purge process fighting other concurrent database operations for resources. If you do decide to keep the default purge process in place, I recommend changing this to a time when the SSIS server is likely to be less busy.

A much bigger issue with the built-in log purge process is the way in which the deletes are performed. The job step for purging this data executes the `[internal].[cleanup_server_retention_window]` stored procedure in the SSISDB database. If you care to take a stroll through the code in that stored procedure, you'll discover that most of the delete operations are performed against a single table, the `[internal].[operations]` table, even though there are dozens of tables that are touched by this delete operation.

The way this works is that the `[internal].[operations]` table is at the top of a hierarchy of tables, bound together by foreign keys. Each of those foreign keys enables the `ON DELETE CASCADE` behavior, which will delete rows in the foreign key table when that referenced value in the parent table is deleted. This hierarchy of tables goes up to 4 levels deep, so you can imagine the inefficiency when this purge process runs, particularly if there is a lot of detail data to be removed.

To avoid this cascading delete problem, I've written a custom deletion script that handles the deletes more efficiently. This script builds a list of execution IDs and executes the deletes using a bottom-up methodology to avoid the costly `ON DELETE CASCADE` process. You can review and download the script here: **TimMitchell.net/go/ssis-catalog-cleanup**. If you choose to implement this script, I'd recommend creating a whole new stored procedure, rather than overwriting the built-in stored procedure, to ensure that future changes to SSIS don't inadvertently overwrite your custom changes.

> ### *What's the best practice for setting up log retention in the SSIS catalog?*
>
> For most, the default 365-day retention period is enough. Having a year's worth of data is more than enough to give you visibility into how each package is performing over time. Keeping that much data also provides you with enough insight to look into more systemic issues impacting more than one operation, such as source or destination systems that are unreliable or slow to respond.

I have found a few recommendations online that a much shorter retention window – as short as 30 days – works better. While I won't argue that a very short window is appropriate for a small number of implementations, my experience with SSIS and ETL in general tells me that such a narrow window of visibility isn't enough to provide a full picture of the health of the ETL operations.

You may also need to keep data even longer than the default retention period. In that case, you could either widen that window, or disable the log purge process entirely. Those cases are rare, however.

Further, you need to be aware of period-end ETL logs as well. If you leave in place the 365-day retention period, you'll only ever have one year-end ETL log data in SSISDB. For environments that have period-end financial close processes, you're going to want insight into at least one past ETL cycle for that close process. If you plan to keep one year of data, I'd recommend changing that to something slightly bigger than 365 days to allow time to compare one year-end ETL cycle the previous one. Make similar adjustments if you keep even less data (such as 30 or 60 days) in your log tables.

You might also consider a hybrid approach, where you keep the high-level information (such as `[catalog].[operations]` and `[catalog].[executions]`) for a longer period while keeping the detail information and messages on a shorter retention window. This allows you to see package-level statuses and runtimes without most of the bloat of the detail information.

Project Version History Retention

As I demonstrated in Chapter 3, the SSIS catalog stores a specific number of versions per project in its history. By default, the 10 most recent versions of each project will be kept in the SSIS catalog. Shown below is the section for configuring the project version retention settings.

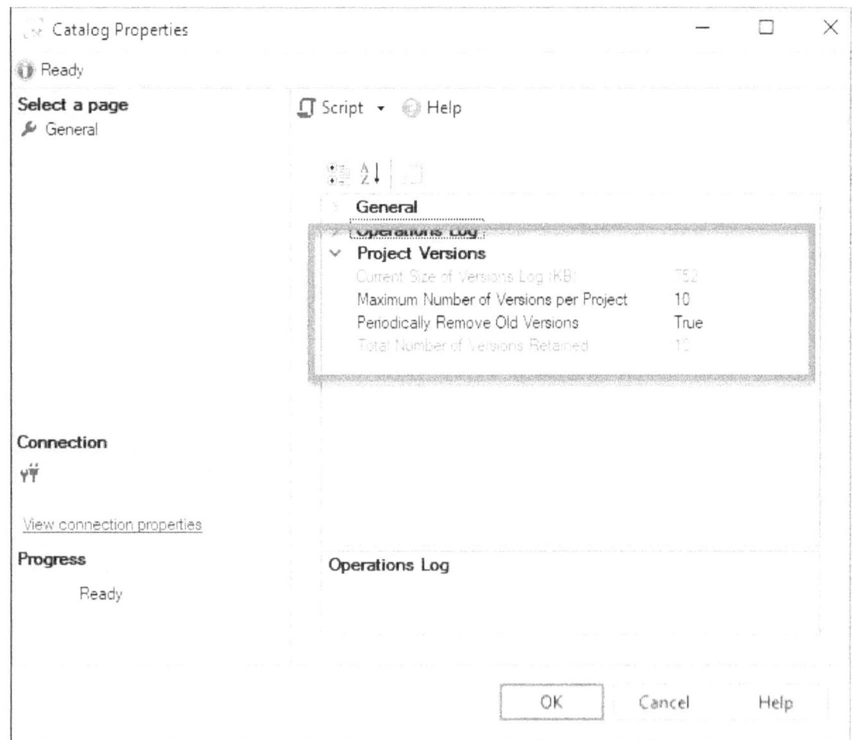

With this feature enabled, a daily process will delete all but the most recent 10 active versions of each project. Note that if you have an older project version that you have marked as the active version, the purge process will not delete that version even if it not one of the newest 10 project versions.

The job that runs this purge is the same job that runs the daily log purge (*SSIS Server Maintenance Job*). This operation is handled through a separate step in that job.

SSISDB Database Management

There is a lot of application logic built into the SSIS runtime, but under the hood, everything that happens in the SSIS catalog relies on the data stored in the SSISDB database. The serialized SSIS objects, folder structure, security settings, and log data are all stored in this database.

As such, the SSISDB database should be treated as an essential enterprise database. Regular backups, performance monitoring, index maintenance, and other tasks common to critical databases are all required and should not be neglected.

The SSISDB database is set to full recovery model by default. Under this setting, a properly backed-up SSISDB database can be restored to a specific point in time for which a backup exists.

If you're unfamiliar with SQL Server recovery models, here's a quick summary of the full recovery model. When using full recovery model, you'll need to set up regular full backups (which back up the entire database), usually on a daily or weekly basis. In between each of those full backups, you'll also need to run transaction log backups, which back up the net changes in the transaction log since the last backup. In the event that you need to restore the database from backup, you would be able to restore the database to a specific point in time by using the most recent full backup and the sequence of log backups.

This point-in-time recovery capability is essential is essential for line-of-business transactional system. However, for the SSIS catalog database, this is most likely overkill. In all my years of working with the SSIS catalog, I've never had a single case in which I needed to do a point-in-time recovery with the SSISDB database.

For most implementations, using a simple backup strategy with daily or intraday full backups is sufficient. When I work with clients on their SSIS architecture, I usually recommend to them that they change the recovery model on the SSISDB database from full to simple to avoid the need to run both full and transaction log backups.

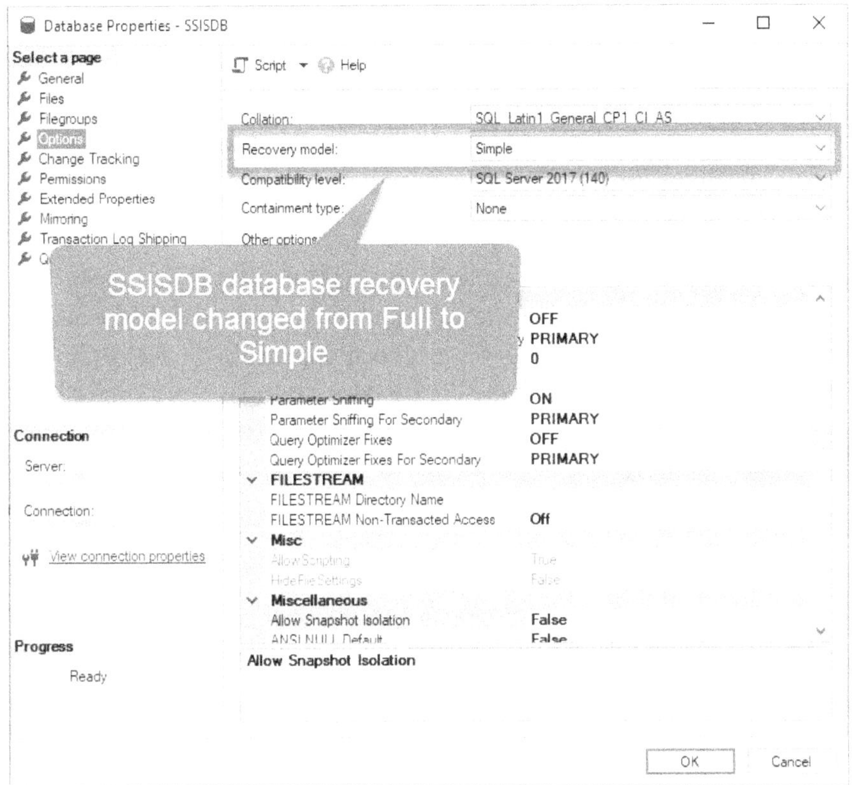

Of course, if your organization has a business case to require point-in-time recovery capability, you can leave the SSISDB database set to full recovery model. If you do this, don't forget to set up log backups in addition to your full backups to avoid uncontrolled transaction log growth.

Restoring SSISDB

Once you have your backup strategy in place, make sure you have a plan for restoring SSISDB. When restoring your SSISDB database, you're likely dealing with one of two scenarios:

- You are restoring SSISDB on the same server, to resolve an issue with either data loss or corruption

- You are restoring SSISDB on a different server, either as a planned move or to recover from a major issue on the original server

Restoring the SSISDB database from backup on the same server is certainly the simpler of the two operations. If you do have a need to restore an SSISDB database to a new server, I would recommend creating a new SSIS catalog (which will automatically create the SSISDB database) and then restore the backup. Doing so will save a few steps, including the creation of the log and version history cleanup SQL Server Agent jobs.

Microsoft has published a detailed set of instructions for restoring the SSISDB database, covering both same-server and new-server scenarios. Since Microsoft's guide on this topic is clear and thorough, I'll just link to it rather than duplicating their instructions. You can find the SSISDB backup and restore guide linked here: **TimMitchell.net/go/backup-restore-ssis-catalog**.

Index Maintenance

Just like any other database, the SSISDB database needs periodic attention to maintain its indexes. As of the SQL Server version used for this writing (SQL Server 2017), there are 230 indexes across 45 tables in the SSISDB database. As these tables are loaded with data, indexes will need to be reorganized or rebuilt periodically to maintain efficient read and write operations.

Maintenance Job Monitoring

As noted earlier in this chapter, there is a SQL Server Agent job named *SSIS Server Maintenance Job* that is responsible for the daily execution of the cleanup operations, including the purge of the log tables and the project version table. Be sure to add this job to the list of operations monitored by your DBA staff, since you'll need to investigate if the job fails or does not execute for any reason.

SSIS Scale Out

Starting with SQL Server 2017, Integration Services came equipped with scale-out functionality. This allows you to set up an SSIS server as a scale out master, and configure one or more workers to which package executions can be distributed. If you have times where several resource-intensive packages need to execute simultaneously, using SSIS scale out can help to distribute the workload by distributing package execution to other SSIS servers.

When installing SQL Server, you'll have the option to configure SSIS to allow the catalog to be used as a scale out master, worker, or both. Once this is installed, you'll need to configure the master and workers separately so that they recognize each other. Because the traffic between the two is encrypted, both the master and the worker use root certificates to ensure security of this exchange.

Jobs can be distributed from master to worker node per each execution, by using the `[catalog].[add_execution_worker]` stored procedure to specify the worker node(s) on which the package may be run. When the package is executed in this way, the logs show up on the master node (not the worker), so you get a single pane of glass for your activity data.

SSIS Scale Out in the Real World

While SSIS scale out is a useful feature, I've found that very few organizations are implementing it. There are a couple of reasons behind this.

First, the scale out functionality was just introduced with SQL Server 2017, so it's still a relatively new feature. Give it some time, and it'll grow in both popularity and in internet culture (blogs, videos, and presentations).

However, the second reason has really been the limiting factor of scale out. Many organizations are shying away from the scale out functionality because of the licensing requirements. The master node for the scale out setup requires the costly Enterprise edition of SQL Server, and each worker node requires a full SQL Server (Standard edition or better) license, even if you are only using that instance for SSIS scale out. Further, if your packages use any Enterprise features (such as the fuzzy lookup or fuzzy grouping), the worker nodes that can execute that package must also have Enterprise edition installed.

> ### *Should I have a dedicated SSIS server?*
>
> In a perfect world, yes, a dedicated SSIS server is ideal. Dedicated hardware and software mean that you can decouple some of the ETL workload from the other operations on that server, and possibly speed up both the ETL and the other processes that would be running on an otherwise shared instance. Since SSIS requires its own memory space separate from SQL Server, isolating the SSIS runtime on a separate server can improve package runtimes in certain circumstances.
>
> However, this type of setup costs more, both in terms of dollars and time. Standing up a dedicated physical SSIS server usually requires more hardware and more licensing costs. Even if you set this up in a virtual environment, there is more administrative work required for an additional operating system.
>
> For modest workloads, a dedicated SSIS server isn't needed. In fact, most of the clients I have worked with are running SSIS on an existing SQL Server used for more than just ETL work. However, if you do hit a bottleneck on an SSIS catalog server on a shared instance, a dedicated server can help. Just consider all the costs before going down that path.

Always On

In organizations where high availability for the SSIS server is a priority, Always On can be enabled on the SSISDB database. This functionality was improved with SQL Server 2016 through Always On support in the catalog itself (not just for the database) to allow for easier failovers.

The process for enabling Always On requires two steps: create the Always On availability group for the SSISDB database, and then turn on Always On support in the catalog. If you're interested in a brief step-by-step guide on setting up Always On with SSIS, you can find that through this link: **TimMitchell.net/go/ssis-always-on**.

SSIS Catalog In The Cloud

Early in its life, SSIS was mostly an on-premises ETL solution. However, since its release in 2005, cloud computing has gone from a footnote in architecture to one of the most common means of spinning up machines and environments quickly.

Even though SSIS, and specifically the SSIS catalog, were not specifically designed for the cloud, there are increasingly easy to use ways to push SSIS workloads to Microsoft Azure or other cloud providers.

SSIS In A Cloud VM

The easiest way to migrate an SSIS catalog to the cloud is to spin up a virtual machine and run it there. By far, SSIS running in a cloud VM is the most common design pattern for moving SSIS to the cloud.

The best case for this is one of simplicity: a cloud-based VM running SQL Server and the SSIS catalog looks nearly identical to an on-prem instance. The advantage of using this design rather than its on-premises cousin is that you can easily scale up, scale down, and even shut down/start up on demand when that machine is running on a cloud VM.

Another advantage of this model is that you are not locked into one specific cloud vendor. Because the catalog runs on a virtual machine, you can deploy the SSIS catalog to virtually any VM capable of running Windows and SQL Server.

The cost model for running the SSIS catalog in a cloud VM is similar to that of an on-premises machine. You'll still need a SQL Server license in addition to the costs to maintain the VM itself. There are also pay-as-you-go options available in Azure in which the cost of the SQL Server license is included in the operational fees for the virtual machine, which can present cost savings if you have an SSIS catalog VM that does not need to be powered on all the time (for example, if your shop only runs loads on a nightly basis).

More recently, Microsoft has enabled Azure Data Factory (ADF) for SSIS package support. The SSIS runtime in ADF allows you to deploy your projects to a virtual SSIS catalog in the cloud. Unlike using a cloud-based VM, there is no Windows machine to manage here; when you spin up an SSIS runtime in ADF, the platform-as-a-service model allows you to quickly deploy and execute packages.

The SSIS runtime for ADF resulted, in this author's opinion, as a stopgap to allow the continued use of SSIS in a cloud-focused Microsoft. When ADF was introduced, there were a lot of public complaints and concerns that the lack of new development on SSIS meant that ADF was the heir apparent to the now "legacy SSIS" architecture. Fortunately, Microsoft clarified the messaging, and reinforced that SSIS is part of the future by allowing not just classic on-prem or VM implementations but support in ADF as well.

In the real world, at least as of the time of this writing, implementations of SSIS on the ADF runtime are very small in number. I've worked with scores of clients using SSIS over the past decade, and I can count on my fingers the number who have implemented the ADF runtime for SSIS. This is a design that I expect will eventually grow in popularity, but for now there are a number of limiting factors:

- The hourly ADF runtime in SSIS is relatively expensive compared to the operating costs of a similarly-equipped VM.

- The ADF runtime is incurring charges for the entire time it is turned on, not just when it is running packages.

- The ADF runtime takes a while to spin up once you turn it on. I've seen it regularly take 30 minutes from enabling to fully available.

- You don't have the same amount of flexibility of local resources (such as custom components or file system access) on an ADF runtime for SSIS as you would for an on-prem machine or cloud VM.

Now don't let me talk you out of using the ADF runtime for SSIS. If you have a modest number of packages and can't or don't prefer to provision a virtual machine, deploying your packages to the ADF runtime can be a good option.

Chapter 8
SSIS Catalog Security

Security is one of the most often overlooked aspects of the SSIS catalog. Some of the most important assets an organization will have are either stored in or are accessible by the SSIS catalog, so it is essential to make sure that the data it contains is properly secured and managed.

When we talk about security of the SSIS catalog, we're usually discussing one of four areas:

- Securing the SSISDB database

- Securing the SSIS catalog

- Managing sensitive values in the catalog database

- Managing the account used for execution of SSIS packages

Each of these is an essential part of keeping enterprise data secured, and should be a key part of every company's ETL strategy.

Securing the SSISDB Database

As mentioned early in the book, the catalog's data is stored in the SSISDB database. As databases go, this is just an ordinary user database, requiring the same attention to security as any of the other application databases in SQL Server.

Database Users and Roles

When reviewing the list of database users in SSISDB, you will find most of the following:

- AllSchemaOwner

- ModuleSigner

- ##MS_SSISLogDBWorkerAgentUser##

- ##MS_SSISServerCleanupJobUser##

- SSISScaleOutMasterUser140

The first four of these are common to SSIS, used for securing the SSIS runtime's internal calls to SSISDB and for managing the daily cleanup operations. The last one on this list would be found if that instance of the SSIS catalog is set up to operate as a scale out master. Fortunately, these database users don't require much maintenance, but you should be aware of their presence in case they come up in a review or audit.

There are two SSISDB database roles that are regularly used for SSIS operations. The `ssis_admin` role is granted access to all SSIS catalog-related operation in the database. The `ssis_logreader` role allows users limited access to catalog functionality, and is intended to permit the execution of built-in SSIS catalog reports.

SSIS Catalog Permissions

The SSIS catalog itself also has granular security settings. SSISDB database security is the broadsword, and the security setup in the catalog is the scalpel. The latter allows you to refine what a particular user or group can and can't do in the SSIS catalog.

Within the catalog, you can define permissions on each folder, project, and environment. These settings, which look a lot like a Windows access control list (ACL), allow you to grant or deny permission to a specific object. Shown below is the Permissions tab for an SSIS catalog environment, in which I have granted a Windows user named ssis_execution_user rights to read but not modify this environment.

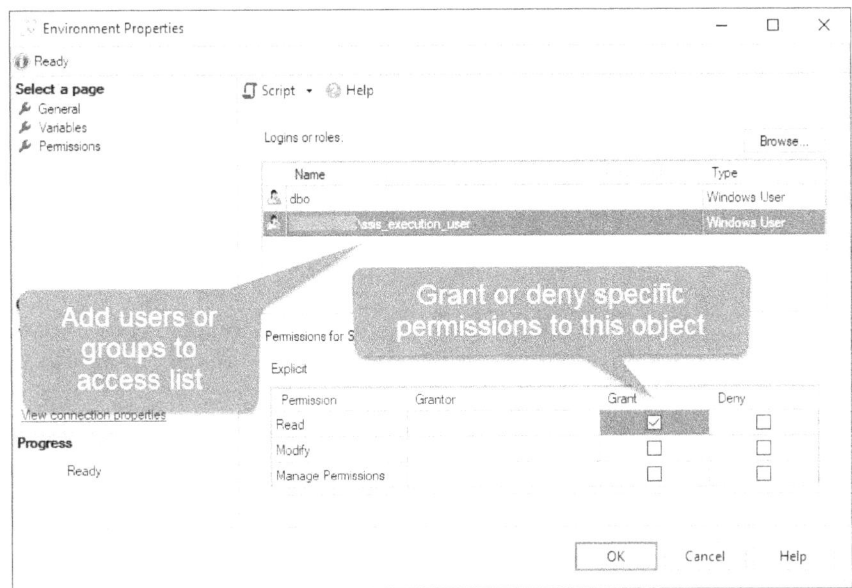

If you browse to the Permissions tab for a project, you'll also see the Execute permission listed as an option.

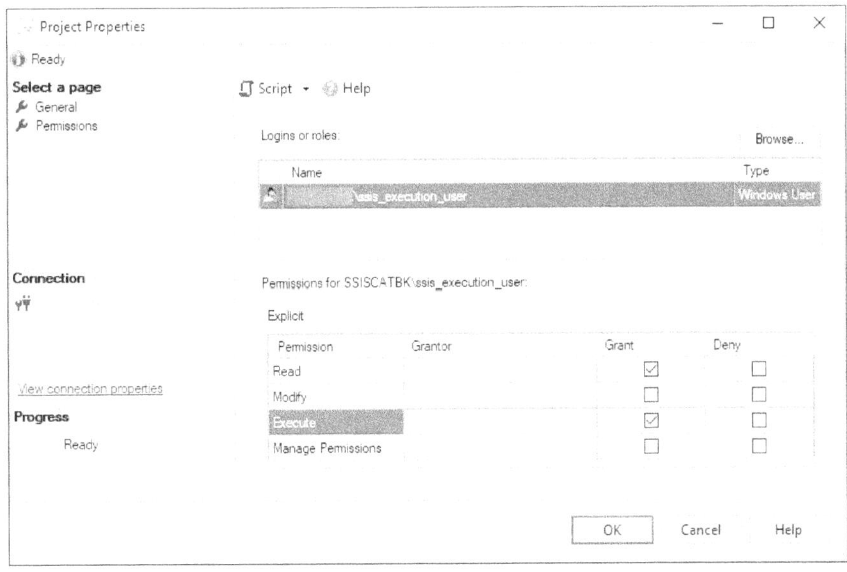

Permission settings on user-created folders in the SSIS catalog are even more broad. As shown, you can grant permissions to the folder allowing read, write, and execute access to all of the projects and environments therein.

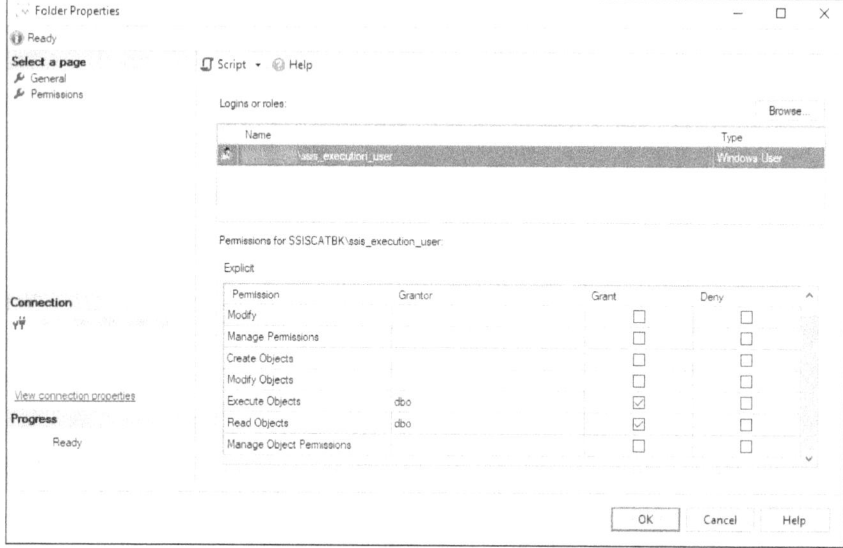

Here are a few things to keep in mind about using SSIS catalog permissions:

- When granting permission to a user or role in the SSIS catalog, make sure that account also has permission to access the SSISDB database. These settings define the application-level permissions, but that user can't do any of these things if they can't first access the SSISDB database.

- Permissions can be set up at the folder, project, or environment level. You'll probably notice that permissions can't be set at the package level – that's by design.

- Just like with Windows permissions, Deny takes precedence over inherited Grant permissions. If you grant folder-level permissions to a user but choose Deny on a project, that user will be denied permission to that project.

Execution Account

The account you use to execute an SSIS package is an important decision, and is unfortunately a frequent point of failure for new deployments. The execution account controls access to file system resources and database end points in many cases, so it's important to understand how this account's permission will impact the execution life cycle.

Why Is the Execution Account Important?

Executing an SSIS package will almost always require access to secured assets: files or folders, relational databases, or email accounts, among other resources. These resources are (hopefully) protected from public access, and the user account used to execute the package is, by default, the security context used to access those resources secured by Windows authentication. If you execute a package that used your Windows credentials, and you do not have access to one of the assets touched by that package, the execution will fail.

Where we often see this fail is when moving from testing interactively to scheduling a package to run automatically. "It worked during testing!" is a frequent complaint about SSIS security.

Which Account Is Being Used?

Let's first walk through a few scenarios to better understand the effective user account.

- Manual execution from SQL Server Data Tools: In this scenario, you're not really interacting with the SSIS catalog at all. During this execution, your local machine is doing all the work, and your Windows user account is the effective user account.

- Manual execution from T-SQL or SSMS: If you browse the SSIS Catalog node and execute a package from SSMS or start a package execution from T-SQL, your Windows account is the effective user account.

- Scheduled execution via SQL Server Agent job: By default, the account used here is the service account for the SQL Server

Agent. Alternatively, you can set up and use a proxy account, which I'll cover in the next section.

There are exceptions to the above. Most notably, if you are accessing a resource that has its own credentials stored in a parameter (such as a database connection with a user name/password credential, or a web service with an API key), the execution account shouldn't impact those connections. However, for accessing any resource that does require user credentials, the effective account is the one that dictates what can and cannot be accessed.

Since most enterprise SSIS activities are run as scheduled jobs rather than interactive operations, we'll focus mostly on that activity.

Setting Up and Using a Proxy Account

In SQL Server terminology, a proxy account is a reference to a user account that can be used as the effective user account for schedule activities. In functional terms, a proxy account lets you specify a different account with which to execute a package from a SQL Server Agent job.

A proxy isn't just an SSIS catalog concept – it's actually part of the broader SQL Server stack and has implementations in other applications as well.

Setting up a proxy is a three-step process:

- Create the credential object in SQL Server. This will bind a specific Windows user account to the credential.

- Create the proxy using the credential created above.

- Grant access to the SSIS subsystem for the proxy. This will allow you to use the proxy in a SQL Server Agent job to execute SSIS packages.

When setting up a proxy, make sure you do so with a nonprivileged Windows account that is not a named user's account. Think of this as being similar to a service account, in that it should be specific to this purpose and should never be used as a machine login account.

Shown below is the script I have used for creating a proxy for use in SSIS package execution.

```sql
/*******************************
Create a credential to be used by proxy
*******************************/
USE [master]
GO
--Drop the credential if it is already existing
IF EXISTS (SELECT 1 FROM              .              WHERE name =
N'ssis_execution_credential')
BEGIN
        DROP CREDENTIAL [ssis_execution_credential]
END
GO

CREATE CREDENTIAL [ssis_execution_credential]
        WITH IDENTITY = N'DOMAINNAME\ssis_execution_user'
        -- Existing nonprivileged Windows acct
        , SECRET = N'SuperSecretPassword'
GO

/*********************************
Create the proxy account and grant access to SSIS
*********************************/
USE [msdb]
GO

-- Delete the proxy if exists
IF EXISTS (SELECT name FROM msdb.dbo.sysproxies WHERE name =
N'ssis_execution_proxy')
BEGIN
        EXEC msdb.dbo.sp_delete_proxy
@proxy_name=N'ssis_execution_proxy'
END
GO

-- Create the proxy using the credential defined above
EXEC msdb.dbo.sp_add_proxy @proxy_name=N'ssis_execution_proxy'
        , @credential_name=N'ssis_execution_credential'
        , @enabled=1
GO

-- Grant access to the SSIS subsystem for this proxy
```

```
EXEC msdb.dbo.sp_grant_proxy_to_subsystem
@proxy_name=N'ssis_execution_proxy', @subsystem_id=11
GO
```

As shown, I created the credential using an existing Windows account, created a proxy using that credential, and then granted that credential access to be used by SSIS.

Once this has been set up, I can now change the execution account on my SQL Server Agent job(s) to use that credential. As shown below, I now have `ssis_execution_proxy` as an option for the Run As selection in my SQL Server Agent job step for this SSIS package.

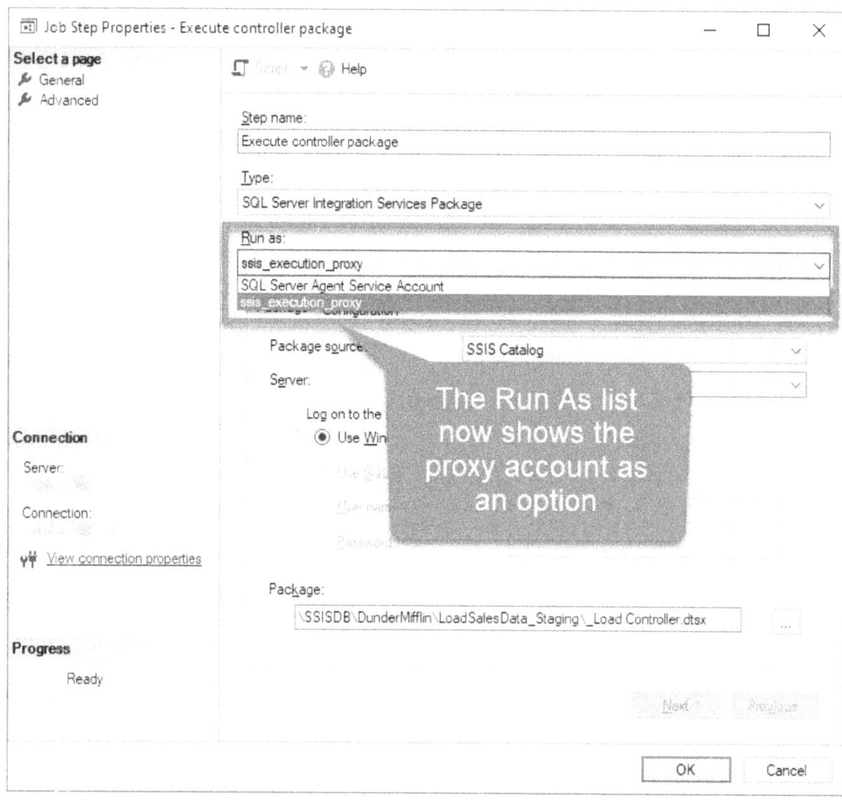

Note that you can set up more than one proxy on each server, which would allow you to limit permissions of each account to only a specific domain of data. In this Run As list, you will see all the proxies on this server that have been granted access to the SSIS subsystem.

Epilogue

In the pages of this book, I have labored to introduce you, dear reader, to the workings of the SQL Server Integration Services catalog. I've done my best to share with you not just the academic summary but my real-world experience as well.

As an author, it is always my sincerest hope that you find these words of use to you. Since I strive to always improve and make vNext better than vCurrent. To that end, I welcome any feedback you have – either positive or negative. Feel free to reach out to me at **TimMitchell.net/Contact** or ping me on Twitter at @Tim_Mitchell.

Don't forget to check the companion website for this book at **SSISCatalogBook.com**. Source code from the examples, errors or clarifications, and other resources will be available there. You can also leave any feedback specific to this book on that site.

Finally, thanks for investing the time to read this book. Your time is the most valuable thing one has to trade, and I'm honored that you've spent it here on my humble pages.